HIRING WITHOUT HESITATION

A How-To for Small Business Success

LAURA NELSON

RIVER GROVE
BOOKS

This publication is designed to provide accurate and authoritative information in regard to the subject matter covered. It is sold with the understanding that the publisher and author are not engaged in rendering legal, accounting, or other professional services. If legal advice or other expert assistance is required, the services of a competent professional should be sought.

Published by River Grove Books
Austin, TX
www.rivergrovebooks.com

Distributed by River Grove Books

For ordering information or special discounts for bulk purchases, please contact Greenleaf Book Group at PO Box 91869, Austin, TX 78709, 512.891.6100.

Design and composition by Greenleaf Book Group
Cover design by Greenleaf Book Group and Mimi Bark
Cover Image: Overhead shot of office desktop with copyspace, used under license from Shutterstock.com/©One Pixel Studio

Publisher's Cataloging-in-Publication data is available.

Print ISBN: 978-1-63299-325-0

eBook ISBN: 978-1-63299-326-7

First Edition

I would like to dedicate this book to three people in this world who have always been there to listen to me and help me find my words.

First, to my parents, Fred and Kathy, who have always been my biggest cheerleaders and gave me the foundation I always knew I could fall back onto at any point in my life: Thank you for all you have done to help me become the person that I am today.

Second, to Chris, the man who has seen my heart from the very first time we met: Thank you for seeing the *real* me and allowing me to peel away the outer shell of my protective onion to uncover what no one had ever seen before. Even me! I cherish you and our life together.

Third, to everyone who reads this book: Thank you, too. I never thought I would write one book, let alone two, and now I feel as though I am just getting started. I dedicate this book to you as well, because I know how hard it is to be a small business owner, but I can tell you it is worth the effort and the sleepless nights. At the end of the day, you believed in something, and you are making it happen. I thank you for letting me be part of your journey.

CONTENTS

INTRODUCTION

I've been in the dental industry for almost twenty years—first as an office manager and now as the founder of a fifteen-person business called Front Office Rocks, which provides the leading online training resource for dental office teams nationwide. What I've learned is that hiring new staff is a daunting, yet surmountable challenge not only for our industry but for small businesses nationwide.

My former husband and I opened our first dental practice in January 2003 outside of Baltimore, Maryland, and were earning more than $120,000 a month in a matter of a few years. In January 2007, we traveled with our entire staff to the West Coast for hygiene training and fell in love with Southern California. We sold our house and our practice and moved across the country with our two young kids.

We opened our second practice in 2008—right during the recession, in a highly competitive dental market and only twenty minutes from Mexico, where patients can go to get dental procedures at a significantly lower price. I've experienced the challenges of starting from zero and getting multiple small businesses to succeed, just like many of you.

Several years on, I'm happy to report that the latest practice in San Diego generates more than $250,000 a month as a fee-for-service office, with an average of sixty to a hundred new patients a month. I hired and managed a staff of more than fifteen people, including three doctors, four RDHs, three dental assistants, and four front-office employees. Due to the growth of my business, I have since moved on from managing the dental office and now fully focus on Front Office Rocks.

Dentistry isn't the only field I know, however. During college, I was an assistant manager at a clothing store chain, and my first job out of college was as a salesperson for a regional trucking carrier. I've also written my first book (*Step Away from the Drill*) on elevating training and customer service, and I've worked as an administrative and technical recruiter for Fortune 500 companies, universities, and other businesses, where I conducted courses and learned the ins and outs of the hiring process. With all this experience, I have learned that there's a lot more to hiring than what an employer wants to pay and what someone wants to earn. It's about positioning your business in a way that is appealing on multiple fronts and using skillfully crafted techniques to find that needle in the haystack to build a great team.

With a BA in human resources from Eastern Michigan University and an MS in organizational development from Johns Hopkins University, I also deliver seminars all over the country to help business owners improve their customer service and systems, experience lower staff turnover, increase their revenue, and receive hands-on office training. In short, I help them become more productive and successful.

I've heard more stories than you can imagine about successful hiring and disastrous firing and have learned firsthand what works and what doesn't. Unfortunately, too often, small business owners, even highly trained specialists in their fields, are not good at the actual process of hiring. The reason is because they have never been taught how to hire someone. In other words, they are ill-equipped or not trained to bring on the new employees they need to grow. I understand. As a small business owner, you often carry the weight of the entire enterprise on your shoulders when you should be focusing on what you do best. You are good at what you do, and when that happens, your business grows. As your business grows, you should be with your customers or patients, and when you're not at work, you should be enjoying the results of your hard work, not fretting about what isn't getting done. But as you get better at effective hiring, the less time you'll spend actually doing it, and the less turnover you'll have.

Especially in a small business, employees are an integral part of your success, and they are more intimately connected to your purpose than those in larger companies. If you understand what you should expect from your team and you have the resources to train them, then the next step is learning how to hire the right people from the start. And that's where *Hiring without Hesitation: A How-To for Small Business Success* comes in.

I'll give you the tools and information you need to find your next great hire. We'll cover everything from assessing your needs to crafting job descriptions, sorting through resumes, conducting interviews, confirming finalists, and training and onboarding your new team member.

In this book, I am going to teach you the process that I use to hire new employees and the steps you need to save time and make the process more productive—and even enjoyable. I'll share real-world examples and give you tips you can apply in your hiring process easily and immediately. I'll also share lessons about hiring mistakes and alert you to red flags and trouble signs.

My goal is for you to learn how to enjoy the hiring process while building a rock star team. And when you have a great team, you can build great things for yourself, for them, for your clients and patients, and for your entire enterprise.

—LAURA

CHAPTER 1

TAKING THE PLUNGE

Many people launch their small business, as I did, because they have an amazing idea or skill they love. We're excited to offer our passion or product to the world, and getting there takes a lot of education, hard work, and perseverance. We spend years dreaming of the full potential, planning for growth, building things from the ground up, and pouring ourselves into our work to make our vision a reality.

We find that as our business grows, the *needs* of our business grow, and to take things to the next level, we must find help and be strategic in order to keep things sustainable. That's usually a sign that it's time to hire. This is the crucial moment when you make the decision to work *on* your business, not *in* it.

Remember that from a business standpoint, if your organization doesn't grow each year, do new things, and increase in revenue, you're actually doing worse because your costs—overhead, payroll, and supplies—increase over time. You may be tempted to think it's safer to keep things the same, but you're doing more than just holding your business back. You're actually reducing its size and minimizing its potential. Many small business owners think that stability and staying the same is a good thing, but if you are not growing and improving, you are getting worse.

It's important to the health and longevity of your business to transform your mindset and think in terms of growth. Your focus should remain on doing more and doing better, even if it takes a while. Growing, adding new team members, and even turning over employees who need to go are signs that a business is doing well. That's how your business will flourish, and the idea of a growing business should be something that makes any business owner excited.

Large businesses and corporations usually turn to their human resources (HR) departments or outside recruiting agencies when it is time to find and onboard the right talent. They have legal departments to vet contracts and keep current with employment laws. As a matter of course, CEOs or C-suite executives may never even meet many of the new hires who come and go unannounced.

For small business owners, however, a lot is at stake. For the purposes of this book, a small business is any business that has at least two employees and is actively hiring without an internal HR or legal department. When the owner or a manager performs the role of HR, it is still a small business, but when employee management becomes a full-time job, the business has graduated to the next level. In today's competitive economy, the effects of employee turnover and substandard work can be devastating to businesses, especially small ones.

When you only have a few employees, they play a critical role in your successes—and failures. They interact with your other employees, customers, clients, or patients and represent your business in a much more personal and immediate way than someone who works in a Fortune 500 company with hundreds or even thousands of employees.

Small businesses generally can't turn to an in-house HR or legal department to handle the hiring process and smooth out any wrinkles. As the owner, you have to wear all the hats, which means you need to know the basics of hiring if you are going to improve efficiencies, scale up, and grow your business for the future.

I've seen small business owners balk time and again at the idea of hiring additional employees. Many know it costs more than $4,000 on average to hire a new employee in the United States, with small business owners spending $1,872 to hire someone new and up to four months searching for the right candidate, depending on the job level.[1] The average cost of hiring the wrong employee was $17,000 in 2017, according to a study by CareerBuilder, and no one wants to be one of the 62 percent of small businesses nationwide that say they made a bad hiring decision.[2] In my industry alone, I know dozens of dentists who have been embezzled from because they didn't know how to hire the right people or put effective checks and balances in place.

Let's take a look at some of the reasons why small business owners may be reluctant to consider making new hires:

Lack of training. Small business owners rarely receive a formal education in management because they learned along the way building their businesses. They're just not sure they know how to actually hire—and fire—employees. Few dentists, for example, receive any business training when it comes to talent acquisition or employee retention. They aren't taught essentials, such as how to build a good team, manage a team well, or transition employees when needed, and the idea of growing their company by increasing personnel can seem daunting.

Insecurity. I've observed that business owners are usually talented in multiple areas but assume they will fall short in terms of the soft skills and techniques needed to assess and hire a new employee. Feelings of inadequacy may cause them to delay or even ignore the task of hiring much-needed personnel.

Anxiety. As business owners, we've all made mistakes and had bad experiences, which can dictate how we react to future choices. Thinking about managing the hiring process can cause anguish, stress, or anxiety, all of which can be eased when we know how to approach hiring in a smart, intuitive way that best addresses the direct needs of our business.

Lack of time. Most of us are busy enough just running the business and trying to stay healthy and survive. Unlike larger businesses, few small businesses have interns or extra support staff who can pick up the slack in day-to-day operations. Many people believe they can hardly keep up with their responsibilities already, let alone invest in training someone new.

While most small business owners "consider talent to be the greatest asset to the success of their business (82 percent)," according to 2016 findings from Monster.com, "the majority believe it can be time-consuming (89 percent) and expensive (70 percent) to find the right person for the job."[3] On top of everything else, the idea of advertising a job, screening candidates, and training a new employee can seem overwhelming. Many owners think that hiring—and hiring right—requires their full attention, but they don't have the time or attention to give to the process.

I'm here to tell you that "hire" doesn't have to be a four-letter word, and you can learn to love hiring and experience it as a positive, gratifying process that launches your business into a stronger trajectory toward its full potential. With the right team, you can build and foster a team of people who love their work, contribute their skills and abilities, are proud of their efforts on your behalf, and represent your organization well.

Hiring is a way to make your business better and is a sign that your business is healthy and growing. And if you understand the key elements, you'll run a tighter ship, be more successful, and bring out the best in yourself and everyone in your organization.

Whether you are a current or aspiring small business owner,

Hiring without Hesitation will provide you with the motivation, tools, tips, and best practices for hiring top-notch employees. I'll show you the steps and strategies to hire candidates with methods that fit your business and needs. Though you'll find there isn't a one-size-fits-all process, you'll gain more clarity on how to tailor the experience in a way that allows you to hire the best candidate every time. I'll also guide you into your first week with your new employee so you can start them off on the right foot, making your life easier and setting everyone up for success.

This doesn't mean everything will always be easy, but it does mean that you'll feel more prepared in your approach. Then, when you find the best match, you'll feel confident that you're on your way to growing your small business into a larger one and appreciate that it was worth all the hard work. Finally, when you have success, you will start to feel more positive about the entire process.

CHAPTER 2

WHAT'S THE JOB?

You may need to hire someone for any number of reasons. Maybe the business is growing, and you need salespeople on the road, talking to prospective clients or running booths at trade shows. Maybe you're getting feedback that nobody is answering the phone or returning calls, so you need a receptionist or customer service representative. You may need to establish or expand your social media presence. Or it could be that you're losing an employee and have a vacancy. When you notice a critical gap in service or performance that isn't being filled, it's time to hire.

The best thing to do is to act when you see it coming. If you can predict this gap is headed your way, don't wait. When a position goes unfilled for longer than your business can truly handle it, you risk putting added stress on your other employees, which results in lower efficiency, productivity, and job satisfaction. In a worst-case scenario, someone may end up quitting if they are asked to handle too much extra responsibility for too long, which means you have not one but two open positions to fill.

Many times, small business owners think it's easier to just take on everything themselves. It's common to think, "I'm better than anybody else at doing this task, and I need to get this done. I'm going to work a couple extra hours at night and not get home in time to be with my family." But that can only last so long.

Another reason not to wait too long to make a hire is that the pressure to bring on someone (anyone!) increases the longer you put it off. There's an expression, "Hire slow, fire fast." A rush to hire often means you overlook key job criteria (skills, references, etc.) or compromise on what you really need. You may settle for someone "close enough" to what you want and cross your fingers that they'll work out, only to pay the price. As *Harvard Business Review* points out, this "bias for speed"[1] can result in hiring employees who are not the best fit for your company. That would be a mistake, and you'd be doing yourself and your business a disservice.

You'll have a more successful hire when you set clear goals and invest time preparing for the right candidate. This will allow you to hire someone with the skills and personality you need, who fits in with your team, and who becomes part of your long-term growth strategy. To do this, it's crucial to take an informal inventory and identify not only the job that needs to be filled but the soft and hard skills that are needed to do it.

Ask yourself: Why do I need to hire? What are the types of tasks that I could delegate to someone else? Where would a new hire fit in on my team? What kind of personality would work best? What skills and education are necessary?

To be honest, you won't truly know if someone is a good fit for your small business until after they've started. It's kind of like dating. You can check off all the boxes—a certain age, lifestyle, geographic area, occupation—but the less obvious things like chemistry and sense of humor are lacking. Once you start spending time together, you'll soon know whether you are compatible or not. Hiring a new employee is similar, but you can put the odds on your side by establishing a framework for a focused search and organized, transparent hiring process.

IDENTIFY THE NEED

What tasks do you need your new employee to perform? In a small business, the answer to that question is not always as cut-and-dried as it is for a large corporation with well-defined hierarchies and systems or for a place like a fast-food chain where employees have specific skill sets or routine tasks. For instance, if the food is not coming out of the kitchen to customers fast enough, an additional cook is needed. In contrast, most employees in a small business are cross-trained, can do multiple jobs as needed, and tend to jump in and get things done even if a task is not in their actual job description. But you can't exactly place an ad for a jack-of-all-trades, can you?

There are two effective ways to identify the role that needs to be filled:

1. **Ask your employees.** By finding out what they like to do most (and least) in their current jobs, you can identify their strengths and preferences, as well as what they would prefer not to do, which could potentially be transferred to a new hire. Your current employees will appreciate offloading these duties, and you can make sure that the new hire is someone who will enjoy and be good at them. (By tapping into your current employees' needs and wants, you also gain information about their professional goals and can develop retention strategies.)

2. **Find out what is falling through the cracks.** The next thing you need to do is determine what is not getting done, or done well, and what will need to get done for your business to grow and flourish. What about answering phones or ordering supplies? Add those items to your list of job duties for the new employee.

What Do Your Employees Want to Do?	What Do Your Employees *Not* Want to Do?	What Is Not Being Done?

CRAFT THE JOB DESCRIPTION

Now, it's time to use the information you've gathered to craft a focused job description that will clearly tell you and the new hire what is expected of them in the role. It is important to write the job description for your internal use and also for the basis of your perfect job advertisement. Don't make it so narrow or specific that you eliminate those who don't meet every requirement but could grow into the position, and don't make it so broad that you have to winnow through hundreds of applications.

Here are some tips:

- **Come up with a clear job title.** Think about how people are looking for a job like yours, and what search terms they might think of. Use precise words and have some fun, coming up with titles such as "Rock Star Receptionist" or "Client Services Team Lead" that signify the duties and scope of the job.

- **Involve current employees.** No one knows what a job entails—or could entail—better than your team. Ask for their input and advice. What is missing? What should be emphasized or left out?

- **Provide a summary description.** Give candidates a sense of the role and how it fits into your organization. What are the core objectives? Is it managerial? Why is the job important, not just for you but for your clients?

- **Give this position room to grow.** Provide not only specific hard skills and technical requirements but also a sense of how prospects can maximize their professional development and grow with the business. Address their potential for advancement, which is sometimes less obvious in a small company. You can say "Fast-growing company needs their next key team member" or "Lots of opportunity to develop from the ground up and grow with the company."

- **Define your business culture.** With a stronger desire these days for work-life balance and other benefits, job seekers are looking for businesses that are as much a cultural and personal fit as a professional one. What is culture? It's a company's vision, values, practices, and people, and it's shaped by everything from the company's history to its office architecture.[2] People want to be inspired and find meaning in their work. Think about what sets your business apart in terms of its mission and what the environment is like for people who work there. This is a great opportunity to communicate your brand. Because small businesses have fewer employees, it's particularly important for job seekers to get a sense of whom they'll be "rubbing shoulders" with every day. Maintaining a positive company culture boosts morale and reduces stress.

- **Double-check everything.** Make sure your description doesn't contain any misspelled words or grammar errors. Check to be sure it is inclusive and non-gendered. Research has shown how some words can signal gender bias in job ads, and gender-neutral language attracts a bigger and more diverse pool of candidates.

By focusing and optimizing your job description, you'll spend less time sifting through resumes later and more time combing through qualified candidates with the technical skills, experience, and personalities who can help take your small business to the next level.

PINPOINT TECHNICAL SKILLS

The more technical the job, the more likely it is that candidates will need specific training or certification in order to be considered for the position. Those types of skills are absolute requirements for certain jobs. For instance, a dental hygienist or an accountant needs to have acquired specific knowledge and degrees in their fields.

I recommend taking an inventory of the technical skills you think will be needed for the role. Think about whether some of the skills can be taught on the job or through professional development courses. Do you need someone who is willing to learn or who is already trained or certified? Small business owners sometimes make the mistake of taking someone off their list who is actually a strong candidate, because they think the person has to come with a certain skill or experience, when really it can be trained or learned.

For example, maybe you use a particular software in your office. Knowing how to use it is a technical skill, sure, but it's also one that can be taught to a new employee. The same goes for knowing how to answer a certain number of phone lines. Honestly, after about five phone lines, does it matter if you have experience with ten or twenty? That makes it a plus, not a true requirement, which allows more people to apply who might have the type of personality that you are looking for.

Make a list of the hard skills you need in a qualified candidate, including those you are willing to teach or have them learn.

Technical Skills	
1	
2	
3	
4	
5	
6	
7	
8	
9	
10	

CONSIDER PREVIOUS EXPERIENCE

Identify the kind of experience you think will be required for the role. This includes both the extent (years) of experience and the kind (types) of experience.

	Experience You Want
1	
2	
3	
4	
5	
6	
7	
8	
9	
10	

Experience can be difficult to quantify, and we tend to put too much emphasis on years of experience versus depth of knowledge. For example, I see job advertisements for a receptionist that require two years of experience answering phones.

That's fine, but do they really need two full years? Maybe they are already extremely good at what they do. Maybe they have the right instincts. Maybe they've done other jobs that prepared them for answering phones. It can be worthwhile to be open-minded and flexible if the candidate looks as if they otherwise might be a good fit.

Consider, for example, someone who was a stay-at-home mom for a year or two. Think about what they did during that time and prior to becoming a parent. Many stay-at-home parents excel at multitasking and managing a household. Did they head up their PTA? Did they run a kids' soccer program or volunteer for a program, perhaps one associated with your industry?

Even if someone doesn't check all of your boxes, they may have other experience that directly applies to the position, and this can make a huge difference for whether they end up on the slush pile or come in for an interview. This does not mean you should throw your door wide open to anyone and everyone, but don't miss out on potentially great employees by adhering too rigidly to your criteria.

ACCOUNT FOR PERSONALITY

In most small businesses, the employees tend to work closely together in an intimate environment. That can be a great thing, for sure, but a productive and successful workplace dynamic depends on having the right personality mix not only for your team but also for the job.

In our dental practice, for instance, we were hiring to help in the front office and had two very organized, detail-oriented people who were not particularly warm or bubbly. They were both awesome employees, but when it came to answering phones and greeting people as they arrived, they were pleasant but very matter-of-fact. I wanted a bit more excitement and energy. For the next hire, I looked for someone with a lot of innate cheerfulness that made people smile when they phoned and visited our office.

Ask yourself: Do you need a strategist? A cautious person? An aggressive one? A team player or someone who thrives on autonomy? Are they enthusiastic? An extrovert or an introvert? With whom do you want to work every day? Do you need someone who is comfortable discussing money, reaching out to clients, or doing cold calls?

Just as important is what kind of person your team wants to work with every day. You might find the best person in the world, but your team may not like them at all. You're not a teacher who introduces a new student to the classroom and then expects everyone to play together. That's not really fair to the new employee, and it's not fair to your team.

Take time to ask your team questions like "What kind of personality would benefit the team? What would enhance our team?

What would make it stronger? What makes someone easy/hard to work with in our office?"

I did this with my team of dental assistants to assess and get buy-in for the next person to be hired. I typically assume that team members who have more experience and have worked with us longer want to hire someone new who is good at following directions and being a team player. But my team told me that they wanted someone with strong leadership abilities and good organization skills.

They said that while they had the best of intentions for organizing their areas and making decisions for the team when things needed to happen, none of them were very good at it. They felt they worked well as a team but could do so much better if they had someone who was a natural leader and could help make decisions and guide their group. I never would have known that unless I asked them, and had I hired someone without their buy-in, someone without that personality style, I am not sure they would have liked it.

Informal Personality Inventory	
1	
2	
3	
4	
5	
6	
7	
8	
9	
10	

SET A SALARY RANGE

It's important to gauge the correct pay rate for your position based on your budget and the market, among other considerations. The amount you can pay will help determine the quality of candidates you attract in terms of their experience and skills.

Unlike big companies, which usually delegate hiring and pay logistics to HR departments or external recruiters, you'll need to find compensation information yourself. A good place to start is by visiting online resources like PayScale, Glassdoor, or Salary.com to review salary and hourly wage data for your industry. The US Bureau of Labor Statistics also offers pay scale information sorted by occupation, state, and metropolitan area.

You also need to consider factors beyond salary, including whether you will have additional expenses to accommodate the new hire, such as new equipment, office space, or furniture. Are you planning to offer benefits such as a 401(k) plan, health insurance, paid sick/parental/vacation leave, or free snacks or meals? Also include items like payroll taxes in your calculations.

Examine your budget and revenue trends and projections, and evaluate your profit margin. To what extent can you support an additional full- or part-time new employee? It may be a good idea to work with your accountant to run the numbers to figure out what value a new hire can bring to your company and what you can comfortably afford. Generally, the low end of a pay range would cover candidates who meet your basic criteria, while the higher end would go to candidates who meet or exceed all of your criteria with little guidance or training necessary. If you can't afford your perfect candidate, maybe there are ways you can compensate for a lower salary with other perks such as flextime, shorter workweeks, or additional vacation. Think about what kind of packages you would be willing to negotiate to bring on someone you want for the long haul.

By following these suggestions and taking the time to focus on what and whom you need, you'll save hundreds of hours when it comes time to select candidates and make your new hire. Keep notes so that these priorities stay top of mind, and don't become desperate if the right candidate doesn't magically appear right away. You want to hire someone—and keep them—knowing you are one step closer to building your team and growing your business.

KEY TAKEAWAYS

- **Identify the need.** *Think about what isn't being done and what needs to be done.*

- **Craft a job description.** *Focus the job on what you want and what you can offer.*

- **Establish criteria.** *Weigh skills, experiences, and personality in terms of what is required and what can be taught.*

CHAPTER 3

GETTING STARTED

Hiring is a complicated process, and it's inevitable that some things will fall through the cracks. But that should be the exception, not the rule. Having a system for hiring that allows for efficiency, communication, and transparency will mean less work for you and send a positive message to prospective employees about how your business treats people.

In other words, you don't need to be a large corporation to have procedures in place that help you bring the right people on board in an efficient and timely manner—and "timely" is key.

Employers are taking nearly twice as long to hire new people as they did a decade ago, which means candidates may move on if you take too long. Applicants want the process to be accessible and fast, and mobility may be limited. If the coronavirus pandemic health crisis has taught us anything, it's that we need to be able to adapt quickly online, to allow candidates to apply easily from their mobile phones or other devices. Limit delays for interviews, even if that means conducting interviews off-hours or integrating interviews via video into your process.

Once you've defined the job and its major responsibilities, stick to the outline. If you've crafted the right job description from the beginning, it will be easier to determine who is qualified and who is not. Getting your ducks in a row prior to posting the ad will hopefully prevent you from feeling overwhelmed when the applications and resumes start pouring in.

Here are some other tips:

- Train your employees to handle inquiries and incoming applications.

- Don't sit on applications too long. Find a system that helps you and your applicants know where they are in the process.

- Ask job seekers about their preferred communication methods.

- Set expectations about the timelines and when they can expect to hear from you.

- Be consistent with your messaging and how you handle applications, but also be adaptive. We have learned things from COVID-19 like the importance of reshaping our business environments. Today, we also have four generations in the workforce, all with different needs, and many people may expect remote work opportunities and work-life benefits to be on the table.

In short, you'll find that the more organized and creative you are, the more you'll attract the right kinds of candidates for the role.

PITCH YOUR COMPANY IN YOUR AD

Crafting an advertisement for your open position is a vital part of recruiting the right candidate, yet many businesses see this step as the most challenging. They forget that the advertisement is exactly what the word says—it is a place where you are *advertising* your opening and your company. It's a sales pitch to get the right candidate interested enough to apply.

Especially in a tight job market, you want to make sure you get the attention of job seekers, or their friends and colleagues, by creating a positive vibe about your business. Candidates who already have jobs are likely not willing to settle for any job that comes along. They're going to wait to apply only when they feel it is a really great fit, and your task is to persuade them that your job will be vastly better than the one they have now.

Most job "ads" are cut-and-dried. They tell you about the job, what you need to do, and what skills you need to have. While it's necessary to include a general job description, you want to focus on selling your business to candidates by communicating your firm's values and mission and how your firm benefits them.

In fact, a study from the University of Vermont showed that ads focusing on the applicant were almost three times more likely to get higher-quality applicants and better matches than ads that focused on what the candidate would be expected to do for the employer.[1] Job seekers were also attracted to ads that included images, another study showed.[2]

Your ad should really sell your opportunity and make people hope that you select them for an interview. They should feel excited about having a chance to work for a great business like yours. Read competitors' advertisements to get a sense of how they are pitching job seekers, so you can analyze what works and can write a better one.

Take a look at the following two ads. Which ad is more appealing and would make you want to apply for the job?

I'm guessing you chose the second ad, and here's why: It speaks to the candidate, not to the job. It uses lively, conversational language and a sense of humor to keep job seekers engaged. It references pay, and it also mentions technical skills but not in a way that could scare off prospective employees.

The second ad also includes some clear specifications but only after giving job seekers a sense of the work environment and culture ("dynamic" and "fun"), and it ends with a strong call to action.

With a longer ad, you can tell your company story, highlight interesting clients or projects, and include anything else candidates might find intriguing. As your business grows, you can use this template for other positions, adjusting it accordingly.

If you are going to use a title with your ad—and I recommend that you do—don't be overly clever or ambitious. I suggest starting with a title that does something more than just describe the position. "Receptionist" and "Administrative Assistant" are straightforward but boring. Instead, you could appeal to candidates' career goals with a loftier-sounding title like "Administrative Executive" or to their personality with "Creative Self-Starter for Administrative Assistant."

What you don't want to do is to get goofy or weird with your titles. For instance, I've seen a trend with dentists who call receptionists their "Directors of First Impressions." I get it. But I would not expect anyone to be searching for this term if they are looking for a receptionist job, and I am not convinced they would even know what it means. It is fine to have unique job titles once someone is working in your office. But when placing a job ad, you want candidates to be able to find it easily.

If you're hiring for a receptionist position, you need the word "receptionist" in the ad. The same goes for an accounting or bookkeeping position, especially because those are the key words that people who want those positions will use to search online. Just try to make your advertisement interesting and exciting as well as clear and informative.

ASK FOR HELP

If you're having a hard time coming up with interesting ideas for your ad, ask your employees what they enjoy most about working for your company. Do you have exceptional benefits? Are you a friendly family organization that celebrates birthdays and anniversaries? Is your location easily accessible by public transportation? Are you in a commercial district with interesting shops and cool restaurants? Are there a lot of opportunities for professional development and career growth? Do your employees feel respected and appreciated?

By the way, this is also a good way to check in with your existing employees to see if they are happy with their own jobs. They may not tell you directly, but you may be able to gauge whether your team is excited that you are bringing someone else on for a particular role and whether they know of someone who might be a good fit for the position.

COMMUNICATE YOUR MISSION

People want to make a difference and play a part in something bigger than themselves, whether it's giving back to the community, taking care of patients, or helping to grow an exciting new company. You want to make clear that your new employee will be part of something beyond their particular role and your office walls.

Small businesses play just as big a role in the world as corporations, if not bigger! Take your cue from these bold mission statements, whether it's Uber ("We ignite opportunity by setting the world in motion"), Kickstarter ("To help bring creative projects to life"), or Life is Good ("To spread the power of optimism").

For instance, I know from working with many dental offices over the years that communicating their mission is frequently not discussed and is a missed opportunity. For a dental office, too, a mission statement that discusses good oral hygiene is far less effective than one that talks about saving lives.

As we get caught up in the daily grind, we often forget the bigger reasons of why we are here. I challenge you to take yourself back to the time when you were studying or training to become what you are now, or when you first had your business dream. What was your reason for starting your business? What was your *why?*

Think about when you were much more idealistic about your business, and put that into words. That is the reason you will attract other great talent to join you.

FOCUS ON KEY CRITERIA

Think back to your inventory from Chapter 2 and what you *need* versus *want* in a new employee. The top needs should go in your ad. If you're hiring an administrator for a hectic business, for instance, you obviously need someone who's a strong multitasker.

Is weekend or evening availability critical? Do they have to have extensive experience with a particular software? Do they need to live locally? Will they have to drive?

It's important to make sure essential job requirements are featured but also are not so extensive that you turn off prospective workers. In other words, you want to set realistic expectations while keeping the door open to promising candidates.

MAKE IT STRONG

Every job advertisement should contain a call to action and make job seekers feel compelled to apply for your position. Everyone knows most employers want a resume, and even then, not all of the candidates follow directions. Encourage them to apply, and give them a little assignment like "Tell us why you are a good fit" or "Put your favorite ice cream flavor in the subject line." This does two things: It shows that they paid attention to the details and suggests that your job is not just one of hundreds to which they have applied.

As an employer and hiring manager, one of my biggest pet peeves is when I receive an email or cover letter that starts with "Dear Sir or Madam" or "To whom it may concern." It doesn't make me feel as though they truly understand or desire the role or were willing to research my company to find out a contact name.

The gift of a good job ad is that it serves as your first screening tool, eliminating candidates who aren't qualified or can't complete even the first step.

Here's a checklist for putting together your job advertisement:

Steps	Completed?
1. Research competitors' ads.	
2. Use an engaging but accurate title for the role.	
3. Use active, creative language to sell the job and your business.	
4. Incorporate feedback from your employees.	
5. Connect the job to your mission.	
6. Focus on the most important requirements.	
7. End with a strong call to action.	

Next, take things a step further and really think outside of the box. If you were someone considering similar positions, what would draw your attention to this one? What else would you need to know? What would you appreciate learning about the role or the company? You can be creative here, but make sure to communicate in an authentic tone that matches your company and culture.

For instance, your office may operate differently or have a culture that is not the norm. Back in the dot-com days, start-ups had to differentiate themselves to attract strong talent, so they added Beer Friday, Ping-Pong tables, and casual work environments to their job ads, and even today, a lot of IT companies do that. At my current company, we all work from home, and I highlight that feature in my job ads to attract the right type of person.

I see this approach all the time on the back of semi-trucks on the highway. Many hauling companies are recruiting for drivers, so they have a permanent sign on the back of their trucks. They highlight things that are important to prospective hires, like the amount they pay per mile or that they pay even if the truck is empty.

REQUIRE A COVER LETTER

A good advertisement instructs candidates to email their resumes along with why they think they are a fit for the position. You'll want the candidates to do that for a few reasons.

The first is to make sure they read the advertisement completely and don't just send you a generic application. You don't want to waste your time on candidates who aren't excited for your specific opportunity.

Asking for a cover letter or specifics in the email also gives you the chance to see if a candidate can follow directions. If they don't have the attention to detail to follow your instructions when they are trying to get an interview, then they are not likely to pay attention to detail as your future employee.

Finally, the personalized request lets you see what the candidate actually has to say about themselves and the job, and how they communicate. A great candidate will write well and make the case for why they can help you (versus your helping them).

You can choose to make the process as easy or as difficult as you want or what you think the job merits, and that can determine how many candidates apply for the position. If you're hiring for a job that is likely to attract hundreds of applications, then you may want to raise the bar and make your call to action a little bit harder with a few additional steps, such as providing a writing sample.

You can also say, "Tell us why you think you're a fit for this position" or "Give us three reasons why you think we should consider you" or "List two reasons why you have the right experience for the job." That way, you can see if they really read the ad, followed your directions, and paid attention to detail.

TIP: HAVE OTHERS REVIEW THE AD BEFORE YOU POST IT

It's always good to have a second, or third, set of eyes. Ask friends, family, or employees to review your ad before it goes live and do the following:

1. **Make sure it's worded well.** Is it interesting? Is it specific enough? Does it adequately describe your company and culture? What appeals to them the most? The least?

2. **Check for errors.** Always make sure to proofread your ad. You don't want to send the message that you are sloppy and unprofessional and don't know how to communicate, or that it's okay for candidates to submit materials with misspelled words or grammatical errors. Your level of messaging helps communicate the level of candidate you want to apply.

TARGET YOUR AUDIENCE

Depending on your industry, budget, and job candidate goals, you have several options for placing your ad on social media or in print (newspapers, newsletters, professional journals, or industry magazines, for example). Broadcast advertisements are expensive and probably not necessary for your small business. While companies may sponsor broadcast programs or buy ads selling their overall services, it's rare to hear or see an ad for a specific position on radio or television.

In contrast, social media sites provide great exposure for little to no cost, giving you more bang for your buck. And you can easily adjust your ad if you need to. For instance, you may decide to reduce the hours, increase the pay, or include more information about benefits. It's generally a good idea to place your ad on multiple platforms for the greatest exposure. At the same time, make sure that your company website has accurate and comprehensive information for interested candidates, and monitor online reviews of your small business to make sure they reinforce the positive reputation you want to send.

The following job sites are the best for small businesses:

- Indeed

- LinkedIn

- CareerBuilder

- Dice

- Glassdoor

- Craigslist

Keep in mind that small businesses may have a harder time finding qualified employees, which means you need to think as creatively as possible about how to get candidates' attention. A January 2018 survey by the National Federation of Independent Business found that 89 percent of small companies had few or no qualified applicants, despite a high unemployment rate, and when big things hit like the coronavirus pandemic, they present even more challenges for employers seeking new hires.[3]

Consider factors like your geographic location. Are you in a small community where word of mouth may be more effective than a formal ad? Do you need someone who knows the area? Maybe your employees, customers, family, or friends can make referrals. Perhaps your small business is in a region with a lot of competitors (think Silicon Valley), or your open position is very technical, and you need help from a talent recruiter to attract candidates from across the country. Is there an industry magazine or trade publication that specializes in the field?

Do you have a college or university in your area, where young people and recent graduates may be looking for part- or full-time work? Trade shows, industry meetings, and other events usually offer ad space in their publications and can be a good place to let people know you are looking for staff.

Typically, the more high-level, specific, or technical the position you're trying to fill, the longer the search. This is not only because your requirements may be extensive but also because it takes more time to spread the word.

I also recommend that you use popular, commonly searched keywords for your online ad. Also regularly update or repost your ad so that it's not buried in online traffic.

There's a lot of content online, and jobs are being posted all the time. It takes some time and active management, but the end result is that your ad will stand out, helping you attract the right person for the job.

DON'T STOP LOOKING

Until the position is filled, keep your ads current and live. If you're not getting enough candidates, the ads may need some revision. Perhaps your net is not wide enough, or you need to get more creative about where to place them.

A prime example of a job advertising challenge in the dental industry right now is the shortage of dental assistants. Placing an ad is often not enough to find qualified candidates or sometimes any candidates at all. Whenever we hire for this position, if I don't get many resumes in the first forty-eight hours, I know it's time to get creative. First, I go back and "beef up" my ad a bit to make it even more attractive, if possible. I then look for more places beyond the regular job boards to run the ad. If I have not already, I post it on all our social media channels and ask my team members to share it with their online networks so that as many people in our industry as possible will see it.

The goal here is not to wait and assume no good candidates exist but instead to make it a game to see what I can do to go out and actively recruit great talent, as if I were playing *Where's Waldo?* I know there is someone out there who wants to work for us. I just need to find them.

Even if you've begun the interview process, there is always a small chance—maybe even a big chance—that you may not find the right candidate on your first round. You don't want to have to start over from square one, and it helps to have candidates in the pipeline in case someone declines the position or doesn't work out. In fact, if you think you might be hiring again anytime in the relative near future, I would suggest not taking the advertisement down even after you hire someone. It is a good thing to constantly recruit new applicants, since you never know what the future might hold.

There are all sorts of reasons why candidates who seemed like a good fit at the start don't seem right in the end. Or you may have employees who need to move on, and you have to replace them unexpectedly. Keep your options open.

SAVE IT FOR NEXT TIME

If your business is growing, this is not the last hire you're going to make, and you don't need to duplicate your efforts every time. You've taken the time to write an effective ad. You've put thought into where and how to post it. I suggest collecting your materials and saving them for reference, whether you keep them in Google Drive or in a folder on your desk.

After you've made your hire, you may hope you never have to go through the search process again. But if your business is successful, you will. And by getting yourself organized now, you're making the task easier for next time.

Okay, now you can hit "enter" to publish your ad. Let the resumes start rolling in!

KEY TAKEAWAYS

- **Create a hiring system.** *Establish procedures that allow for efficiency, communication, and transparency.*

- **Remember your ad is your advertisement.** *Use your job ad to sell your small business culture and benefits so qualified job seekers are excited to apply.*

- **Spread the word.** *Get creative about ad placement and actively manage your ad to keep it in front of prospective candidates at all times.*

CHAPTER 4

CASTING THE NET

When small businesses have a job opening, too often, they just post an ad and hope the right candidate sees it and applies. This does happen but not always, so you should always actively look for potential candidates, on and off the beaten path.

The perfect candidate may already be employed or not be looking for the exact position you've advertised, when they would actually be a great fit for the job. That's why it's important to communicate your opening or desire to hire to others in your own business, industry, and elsewhere. Expanding your net increases the odds of finding someone who is the right fit.

THINK ABOUT CURRENT EMPLOYEES

As small business owners, we tend to wait until we're desperate before we hire or promote. One of the easiest and quickest ways to fill such vacancies is by promoting or reassigning an existing employee and then hiring somebody to replace them in their former position.

No one knows your small business like the people who already work there. And unlike larger corporations, they are more apt to understand how the whole business operates rather than just their particular sphere of responsibility. Your existing team has gotten to know you well, and they have a good sense of the work environment and culture, which is equally important.

The upside to this is that your current employee has already built a relationship with you and your business and seen you through some tough times. Generally, it will cost less time and money—and hopefully, incur less risk—to bring them into a new position that fits your needs and their career goals.

Sometimes small business employees may not feel there is ample opportunity for growth, and that's because we tend to pigeonhole people. Develop a culture that allows employees to grow, take initiative, assert themselves, and cross-train so they can readily step into more responsibility and newer roles.

If you have the right candidate within your business already, chances are that they can move smoothly and seamlessly into a new role. This move allows your business to have more stability in the short term. It also might allow you to make your new opening easier to fill since it is a lower-level position, and your current employee can help train a new one.

On the other hand, not all employees may be ready for a promotion. Just as you shouldn't blindly hire someone referred to you or because they're a family member or a friend, you also shouldn't fill a position from within your business unless you are certain the person is a good candidate and you genuinely see potential in them. Do they have a positive attitude? Have you seen them solve problems and work as a team player? What are their strengths? Their challenges?

Don't create a scenario in which the person won't thrive because they haven't been set up for success or, worse, you end up having to fire them, or they quit. Then you'll have two vacancies you need to fill.

Remember: Just because an employee is good at their job, it

doesn't mean they necessarily want to move to another job or are qualified to do the open job within your business. If you move or promote someone who is not happy about the new role or qualified to take it on, you may end up losing a valuable asset and creating more problems for your business down the line.

To help you navigate this path, ask interested employees to submit a request to be considered, and conduct interviews, much like you do with a new candidate. When I ask current employees why they want the open position, I don't want to hear things like "Because I've been here for two years" or "Because I do" or "Because you have nobody else." Their reasoning should be as clear as if they were applying without knowing me. I want them to discuss their skills, experience, knowledge, and education—tangible reasons for wanting to make a change in the business. If I feel that they should be considered, I put them into the mix of options with the other potential candidates.

ASK FOR REFERRALS

Good referrals can come from good employees, customers, clients, and others, and research shows employee referrals especially boost the odds of a good match more than any other source.[1] It's a great idea to ask your team members to spread the word about job openings on their social networks. If they enjoy working for you, then it's more than likely their friends and others already think highly of your business.

In fact, when posting any business content on your social media, take the opportunity to share a little bit about your team or something fun that you're doing. Without explicitly calling for job applicants, you can highlight unique things about your company, such as community outreach, to let more people know about your company culture and mission.

A colleague of mine who runs a dental office in Las Vegas actually has a waiting list of people who would like to be considered to work in their office. He has people reaching out all the time because the business has a great reputation and its employees love working there. Their amazing culture, which includes team members sharing information on their social media networks and a willingness to accept resumes on a rolling basis, means they very rarely have to run an ad when it is time to hire. They are very confident positions can be easily filled as the practice grows.

The office also hosts a quarterly open house for community members to visit and meet the team. It's not just about scouting talent but about making sure the community knows about their positive culture and work environment.

I've also built a brand and reputation with my current business that reflects an ethical, fun, easy-to-work-for company, which other dental professionals look to for advice and guidance. Front Office Rocks always has people from all over the country submitting their resumes based on our reputation in the industry, our social media presence, and our work culture. We have a folder of candidates who sought us out and told us they would love to be considered when we are ready to hire again. Not only is that a nice pat on the back and a sign that as a business owner, I must be doing something right, but it also gives me the confidence to know that I can pull from a pile of candidates when the need arises. As a result, I don't stress over the idea of hiring.

In your small business, when you tell employees that you're looking for a new hire, be sure to focus on positive attributes that reflect well on them. You can say, "Hey, we're looking, and we would love to have more employees who can multitask and motivate others as well as you do." You can also offer rewards for successful referrals, such as cash bonuses or extra vacation days. You might want to consider creating a how-to guide and developing an easy and transparent system for tracking referrals and rewards to encourage employee participation and enhance your hiring system.

When you value your employees and show them you care about and respect them, they're more likely to want to contribute in positive ways with greater impact than they might have in a larger corporation. And that, too, helps grow your business.

The caveat to this is making sure your current employee understands that no favoritism will be shown to their friend or acquaintance and there are no guarantees the referral will be interviewed or hired. You want to be sure, too, that their relationship outside of the office will not negatively affect or complicate team dynamics or productivity inside the office. If you choose not to interview or hire the referral, make sure you are transparent and don't damage your relationship with your current employee.

SPREAD THE WORD

The people served by your business are among those who know and trust your business the most and are more likely to understand its culture and mission. They might also have friends, family, or other contacts looking for work, and you can feel free to ask them to let others know. Word of mouth, especially on social media and at group gatherings, is a powerful hiring channel.

Clients themselves might be a good match for your job opening. They might not even have considered working for you, but if you carefully reach out to them, gauge their potential interest, and let them know you thought of them specifically for the position, they might end up deciding to apply. In any case, they'll be flattered you asked and happy to hear that you are doing well enough to expand your team.

I have a great example of when this worked out beautifully. I mentioned that we were hiring to the salesperson who provided credit card processing services for our dental office. She and her whole family had ended up becoming our patients, and when I told her I needed a detail-oriented person to help us organize the insurance side of our practice, she referred her daughter to me. I hired her daughter, who worked in our dental office for a few years and still works for me part-time after she decided to work from home while raising her kids.

That said, make sure you truly believe the client could be a solid fit for your business, and consider whether you are willing to risk losing them as an employee—and potentially, as a customer—if things don't work out. Be clear that you are not guaranteeing them a job and that you hope no matter what happens, they understand you want to make the right decision for both of you. It's a risky proposition, so think long and hard before you act.

BE OPEN TO CHANCE ENCOUNTERS

You never know when you might come across your next hire. You might meet someone with excellent skills and a positive attitude working in retail, a hotel, banking, a restaurant, or another service-oriented business. If they're working unpredictable shifts, including nights or weekends, for low pay, they might jump to apply for a job with regular hours and benefits. They might also be drawn to a business like mine in health care that provides a worthwhile community service. We take care of people, making our mission an attractive one.

By keeping your options open and always looking, you can find someone with the intangible customer service skills that are difficult to teach and then train them in the more technical aspects of your specific industry.

For instance, a friend who owns a small business in a small town in Washington State mentioned a vacant office manager position to her bank teller in case she knew of anyone who would be a good fit. At the time, the teller was happy with her current job, but the next year the bank was sold to a large corporation. When the teller became unhappy at work under the new corporate structure, she reached out to my friend, who hired her.

It might feel awkward mentioning an open position in your business to a stranger, but it's really as easy as telling them that you are impressed with their service and giving them your card or contact information. At the same time, you can encourage them to spread the word that you are hiring. Be sure to return the favor by letting people in your network know about the great service you received at the business where you met this person. That's not only the right and professional thing to do but also good public relations for you!

REACH OUT TO PROFESSIONAL NETWORKS

Leveraging your professional network is a great way to find new hires because they know your industry and are likely to have a strong sense of what you need. Attend conferences and take time to meet with peers in person over coffee or lunch to discuss the types of roles for which you're seeking to hire or will likely hire as your business grows.

Your professional network probably knows your competitors, and others who work in the industry might have suggestions for your company. In addition, they may know of qualified people who are considering leaving their jobs.

I hired a sales representative who worked at another business this way. He told me he was about to be relocated, and I said, "Hey, if you're ever in another dental office or you hear about somebody looking for a job, we're actually hiring. Please feel free to give out my email address. Tell them to send their resumes to us."

That night, he reached out to me and explained that he didn't want to relocate with his business because he had small children. He interviewed with us and was a great fit for our position. You never know what might work out.

I do not recommend, however, that you actively recruit—or "poach"—people from a competitor or another small business. Of course, adults can make up their own minds about where they want to work, but it can be construed as unethical and harm your professional reputation. Without realizing it, you may also be asking them to break a contractual agreement, which may contain a noncompete clause. Though such clauses are more common in big business, they can lead to litigation. It's usually not a great idea to initiate conflict with a competitor or step on their toes, especially if you work in the same community and there is enough business to go around.

If you do consider the current employee of another local business or competitor, be sure you find out why they want to leave, and look for potential red flags. Are they interested in leaving because they need more challenging work or because they had poor performance reviews or lack particular hard or soft skills? Do they bad-mouth their current employer (which makes them likely to bad-mouth you)? Are they sharing confidential information about their employer (again, which makes them likely to share yours)?

I recently spoke to a friend who owns a dental marketing company. A person who worked for a dental supply company reached out to him looking for a new job in marketing. The dental supply company was one of my friend's biggest referral sources, so he did not want to burn that bridge; at the same time, this employee would be a great addition to his team.

He was very up-front with the candidate about his concern, and she explained that she had hit the ceiling at the supply company and was going to leave to move into marketing, whether it was with his company or another one. They decided that honesty and open communication was the best policy, so she spoke to her current boss about her plans and desires. Though he was not happy about her leaving, he gave his blessing, and my friend hired her. Their arrangement still allows her to do some side work with her former company to help them out as needed, and she was blessed to move on in her career. In the long run, it worked out for everyone, and no bridges were burned.

Be cautious with references, too, if you are seeking hires from within your professional network. Word gets out quickly, and you don't want someone to counter your offer to a top candidate with a better one or to actively discourage people from applying for your opening. Use discretion while actively searching and tread lightly.

KEY TAKEAWAYS

- **Incentivize employees.** *Create a business and culture where employees will not only consider taking on new roles themselves but also be willing to spread the word about job openings to others in positive ways.*

- **Keep your options open.** *Your newest hire may be your bank teller or your waiter, so be prepared to tell them about your business and what you can offer.*

- **Cast a wide net.** *Use social media and connect in person with your clients, customers, friends, family, and professional network to generate valuable referrals.*

CHAPTER 5

THE PAPER CHASE

Many small business owners feel overwhelmed by having to sift through dozens, or perhaps hundreds, of cover letters and resumes. But if you've crafted a focused, engaging advertisement, placed it well, and spread the word, then chances are you will have a reasonable number of qualified candidates to choose from.

Now it is time to put the final touches on your hiring process, if you haven't already. Knowing that you have a system in place (see Chapter 3) and just need to follow some strategic steps to choose top candidates will help put your mind at ease and take the stress out of the screening process.

It will also help you avoid any confusion and missteps when it comes to providing job seekers with a communicative and transparent process that leaves them with a good feeling about your business, whether you decide to hire them or not. Remember that the process of looking for a job can be as frustrating sometimes as trying to hire a new employee, so the more you communicate clearly with candidates about the process and their status, the better it will be for them, too.

Especially when you're a small business, the way you treat people can build or break your reputation, and you never know when you'll cross paths with prospective hires again.

REVIEW APPLICATIONS

Sifting through cover letters, emails, and resumes is just one of many steps of a complex hiring process, but it's not one that requires as much effort as many people think. Because you likely don't have training in how to quickly read through resumes and may not trust yourself when it comes to judging candidates by their paperwork, you may be tempted to spend equal time on each one. Don't.

Instead, look for key criteria to determine if you should move someone forward in the hiring process. Use their cover letter or email as a general guide or key to their personality, and look to their resume for proof points or as a factual summary of achievements. References and background checks will provide you with more information and confirmation of how you feel about your candidates later in the process.

COVER LETTERS

The cover letter or email is a candidate's calling card, and it's often your first impression of them unless they are a current employee or someone you know. Before email communication, a cover letter was included in an envelope with the resume. Now, a personalized email may be considered the cover letter, depending on the level of your position. For a lower-level position, an email can replace the official cover letter; however, higher-level positions require a more formal cover letter. Regardless, the cover letter will give you an indication of the candidate's professionalism and "soft" social skills, and it will help you understand how someone is likely to approach a task. Do they follow instructions? Can they organize their thoughts? Are they detail-oriented?

Consider meeting someone for the first time. Whether consciously or not, you evaluate how they're dressed, what their body language conveys, whether they have a nice smile, and if they're polite. Sometimes your gut tells you something, and it may be the same with the cover letter, especially if it has a coffee stain or lots of typos!

The cover letter sets the stage for the resume. Here are some things to look for:

- Does the cover letter contain a generic greeting like "Madam," or "Sir," or did they do their homework and research you and your company to find the right recipient, title, and address?

- Does it contain typos or spelling and grammar mistakes?

- How would you characterize the tone? Professional or too casual for your business? Interested and excited, or dull and impersonal?

- Which skills and experience have they chosen to highlight, and are they relevant to your advertised job?

- Have they provided full contact information?

- Were they clear about how their experience connects with your need?

- Is the cover letter memorable in a positive way? In a negative way? Why?

The answers to all of these questions matter. The *degree* to which each one matters, however, depends on you and your business needs.

Personally, I value the importance of a candidate taking the time to at least use spellcheck on their computer before they hit send.

These days, there's no excuse to send something with misspelled words. It just seems lazy and rushed. I would be very concerned that someone would do the same thing to our customers, which would not be acceptable.

At the same time, I don't mind if they personalize their cover letter to make it stand out in a way that is maybe not quite as formal as other employers might like. For example, if they put in their resume something about why they would be a "rock star" employee, I would welcome it because my business is all about building rock stars. Other business owners may prefer a more formal approach, especially if they are hiring for a professional position such as a lawyer or an accountant.

Doing their homework

Many candidates don't even take the time to write a cover letter or personalized email, and send in their resume without researching you and your business. Or they think it's better to apply quickly to be one of the first candidates instead of personalizing a thoughtful cover letter specifically for you.

Remember: You are looking for a candidate who wants to work for your business, not someone who just wants any job. If a job seeker appears to have done their research, it's probably safe to assume they are not just responding blindly to multiple job postings and are actively seeking a particular role with your small business.

The first clue usually lies in the words following "To" or "Dear." Did they address their cover letter to the correct person, with the right title and address, or did they use a generic introduction that shows they didn't do the necessary legwork? Even worse, did they reuse a cover letter and forget to change the recipient name and address from the last job to which they applied? If it's the latter, I think that shows someone is not willing to put in even minimal effort on a routine task.

A cover letter sent to a small business, in particular, should also show that the candidate understands your culture and values. Personal compatibility is important in the close work environment of a small business, compared to a sprawling corporation with hundreds or thousands of employees. It's also important in remote work, where your team needs to be able to get along virtually and the risk of miscommunicating is higher.

Dotting their i's and crossing their t's

Following directions is a fundamental part of any job, whether someone is an entry-level worker or an executive in the C-suite. Did they send you the cover letter in the way you requested, electronically or by regular mail? If it's an email, did you provide instructions for the subject heading, and were they followed? Does the cover letter contain information you requested, such as contact details, willingness to relocate, or a desired salary range? Do you know when they can start?

If your vacant position requires a detail-oriented approach or a focused attention on customer service, then you want someone who at least takes the time to send a cover letter the way you asked them to.

Also, if the cover letter contains typos or spelling mistakes (even one), is this really someone who will represent your business well? These errors, minor or not, show that either they are lazy or they didn't take their application seriously enough to proofread it—or ask someone else to. Mistakes happen, of course, but they really shouldn't happen in a cover letter or a resume.

WHEN A COVER LETTER ISN'T NECESSARY

While cover letters are helpful in the application process, they may not be necessary in all cases. Depending on the applicant and the job, a cover letter may not be something you need to consider.

If you are considering an existing employee or were presented with a candidate through some other means than an ad—perhaps they are a referral from one of your employees, or you mentioned the opening to someone and they sent you their resume directly—a cover letter is not always necessary. These could still be great candidates; they just may not have had an opportunity to read the advertisement, and you already have some kind of a personal connection to them. The lack of a cover letter, in and of itself, doesn't mean you need to eliminate them, especially if they appear to have strong credentials. Use the cover letter as a potential resource to guide you, but there is no one-size-fits-all rule.

RESUMES

While resumes do not hold the magic key to finding perfect employees, as some people believe, they are effective tools in your screening toolbox.

From the candidate's point of view, sending a resume signals their interest in a job and their qualifications. From the hiring manager's point of view, a resume is a way to help identify and rank top candidates and to rule out people who are obviously not a fit for the job.

If you think you'll find your next employee solely via resumes, you may end up making a hiring mistake. That's because there is no way that you can know from a piece of paper the most important information about a potential candidate, including their personality, work ethic, personal drive, or life goals. The only way to learn these things is by getting to know someone personally.

But if you know what to look for when assessing a resume, you can make better choices up front about who will get that opportunity.

The process of elimination

You may have already ruled out some candidates based on their cover letters. For the rest, it's important to have an organized way of sifting through their resumes and deciding who will, who will not, and who might move forward in your hiring process.

It's a good idea not to let applications stack up. The longer you avoid looking at them, the greater the chance that your next great employee ends up being someone else's next great employee. Good people don't stay in the job market very long. You also don't want to give yourself such a daunting task that you burn out going through the resumes and risk making poor decisions by overlooking good candidates and failing to reject bad ones. Everyone's judgment suffers with fatigue.

I sort through resumes in the following way:

1. **Create a folder for incoming materials.** As the resumes come in, I move them into a designated folder in my inbox so that they don't distract me from other projects.

2. **Allot time every day to reviewing resumes.** By doing a little bit each day, I keep resume reviews more "bite-sized" and manageable, and I can approach each one with a clear head.

3. **Decide whether to move forward with certain candidates.** I quickly scan each resume and decide if they are a YES, NO, or MAYBE.

When I developed this process years ago, I received most resumes and cover letters in the mail and had file folders to store them.

Today, applications are nearly always electronic, so I sort them into folders in my email inbox. You can print them out if you prefer to have hard copies.

It may also help to establish a rating system for resumes based on your job criteria. This process can help you identify the very best candidates and also differentiate between candidates whose resumes put them somewhere in the middle. For example, if you have a lot of resumes scored between 6 and 8, you may decide the range is 5 to 7 for a MAYBE and 8 to 10 for a YES. It's also a good idea to jot down any questions about their experience, job history, or other issues that immediately come to mind directly on the resume in case you decide to pursue an interview.

What to look for

Resume writing is an art, not a science. That said, there are a few basic elements you should expect to appear on a promising candidate's resume. These markers can help you assess whether they have the skills and experience you need and any other qualifications you want.

Professional resumes generally contain information that falls into the following categories: work experience, education, skills/knowledge/accomplishments, personality traits and values.

Work experience and education can factor together in your decision about whether to take the next step with candidates. For instance, if someone has a lot of hands-on professional experience in a role similar to yours, or in the same industry, their level of education may not be as important, and vice versa. While resumes tend to be fact-based, candidates may give you clues to their personalities by the way they organize and write about their experiences, and if they include personal information such as hobbies and interests or life goals.

I remember one candidate whose resume I received and typically would have passed on because she had not worked in the past two years. However, she addressed it immediately in her cover letter, which made me take a second look. She did not just say that she was home with her children but instead discussed how she led volunteer projects and started a home business on the side while raising her kids. She told me about the money her volunteer position raised for philanthropy, as well as about the numerous events that she planned. She gave specifics about her volunteer efforts and detailed her home business. I was immediately drawn to her understanding of how to get things done, and that drove me to interview her. She is still working for me today and is one of my most productive employees.

THE NO PILE

In general, it's safe to delete or throw away resumes from people who are obviously not a fit for the position, or any future role. It takes me about a second to read and toss these aside. However, if you think someone's skills and experience may fit another role in your business down the line, it's not a bad idea to hold on to their resume for future reference. You never know.

Which resumes merit rejection? To me, they are the ones belonging to candidates whose skills and experiences are not even close to my advertised job. If you're applying to be my receptionist and worked twenty years in a coal mine, you are not going to make the cut. And if you're applying to work in my coal mine and have twenty years as a receptionist, that won't work, either.

Another resume that's going to land on the NO pile is one that comes from a person who demonstrates a lack of basic skills or a disconnection between the skills I need and the skills they say they have. If I'm seeking an IT professional or social media expert, for instance, I'm less likely to consider someone who wants to fax me their resume.

I'm also not going to second-guess myself. The minute those resumes land in the NO pile, they should stay there. Choosing to reconsider a rejected resume means wavering on your commitment to finding the rock star employee that your office deserves. Although this may seem harsh, keep your eye on the ball and spare yourself the time and energy of interviewing candidates who won't work out.

THE MAYBE PILE

These resumes don't have any of the huge red flags that would automatically land them in the NO pile, but they're also not an obvious YES. For these candidates, I move them to a pending folder to review later more in-depth. I may want to spend a little more time going over their employment history, or I may make some notes about specific concerns to be addressed if I decide to call them for an interview.

I don't spend a lot of time with MAYBE resumes during the initial review—the goal is to quickly drop them into that folder and move on. Why? Because if I am spending a lot of time looking at MAYBE resumes, I may end up losing out on a YES candidate that I have not discovered yet.

The MAYBE pile is reserved for candidates that you're not sure about. They may not have all of the experience you're looking for or maybe there is a big gap in their work history that could be a red flag. Perhaps they followed through on what you told them to do during the application process, but their experience is slightly below what you need but could benefit you in other ways. In any case, I recommend reviewing all of the resumes *first* before returning to consider the ones that fall into this category.

THE YES PILE

I know a YES resume when I see it and I act on it immediately. What does it look like?

First, the candidate has followed my instructions. Second, the resume has all the necessary elements without any concerning gaps or red flags. Third, the candidate has taken care to tailor their experience and skills to my job posting. Fourth, they have included information that speaks to their personality or values, which seem aligned with my small business. And fifth, I have a gut instinct that this person could be my next hire.

For example, when I was a technical recruiter trying to fight for the talent everyone was looking to hire, if I didn't see any huge red flags on a resume, it became a YES immediately. I do that now when I hire for difficult-to-find talent in the dental industry, such as a new dentist and dental assistants. If I start to nod my head or smile a little when I am reading a resume, I act on it because I know the candidates who seem to be a great fit are few and far between. I also know good candidates find jobs fast.

It's important to note that while I create stacks of NOs and MAYBEs, I absolutely do not create a pile of YES resumes, which would almost certainly mean losing out on great candidates by wasting time in the review process. Instead, when I find one that is a clear YES, I pull up my list of questions and call that candidate before they are offered another opportunity. If the candidate answers the phone, I immediately ask whether they have time to talk now or if I can schedule a time very soon to conduct a phone interview with them. If not, I leave a message asking them to call me.

I then place that YES resume in an easily accessible folder, including a note with the date and time when I left a message. When they call back, I'm able to quickly grab that folder and talk through their resume during the interview.

I note the date and time I called because I want to see how long it takes them to call me back—hours, days, or weeks. For me, this person has moved to the "active consideration" process, and the speed of their return call (along with how their voicemail message sounds) is one of the first things I take into account.

> I can't emphasize this enough: Always call the YES candidates. If you end up with a huge pile of them and the prospect of calls seems overwhelming, then either you've let them stack up for too long or you aren't screening them well enough. You should go through resumes daily or every other day if you're actively hiring. The pile should never get so big that you dread having to pick up the phone.

Calling a candidate right away also helps because you can determine the number of in-person interviews to be arranged, based on your preliminary interviews. Depending on those numbers, you can decide whether it's necessary to review the MAYBE resumes again. You may want to enlarge your candidate pool to include a few of the stronger candidates in that category, or you could hold off for now, saving them in case the YES interviews fall flat.

When you quickly rule out the NO resumes, set aside the MAYBE resumes for later review, and stop everything to immediately contact the YES candidates, you make less work for yourself. Most important, you won't have to kick yourself for waiting too long and letting the great candidates get away.

WEIGH THE PACKAGE

Taken together, resumes and cover letters can hurt or help job candidates, and it's important to take both into consideration in your hiring process if you have them.

Ideally, they reinforce the candidate's experience and skills and provide a whole, consistent, and compelling picture of the person's work history, values, and goals. On the other hand, it's critical to see whether there are any problematic issues, such as conflicting information or concerning gaps that aren't covered by either document. You should be able to consult a candidate's resume to see if it backs up what they say in their cover letter.

The combination of cover letter and resume can especially help when it comes to evaluating your MAYBE candidates. For example, let's say I have somebody who I think has potential. Maybe this person is really overqualified for my receptionist role based on their resume, but in the cover letter, they provide a compelling reason for their interest in the job. If they explain this in a way that makes good sense to me, I might actually move the candidate into the YES pile.

Similarly, if I thought highly of a resume but the cover letter contained a lot of spelling errors, the candidate would land on the NO pile. And, as I've explained, a resume and cover letter together can help you weigh education vis-à-vis experience, among other factors. The two documents should give you a complete picture so you can make an informed decision, one way or the other.

Along the way, it's a good idea to write down comments and questions while they are fresh in your mind as you review applications. Start highlighting things that you think are great and want to hear more about, and note issues that are red flags to be addressed if the candidate moves ahead in the process.

For instance, is there more than a one-year gap in a candidate's employment history? Did they graduate/receive their degree? Is a specific experience or skill particularly impressive? Did you read their cover letter and think, "Wow, this is really cool!"?

With so many resumes and cover letters to review, you want to be sure that you cover all the bases when it comes time for interviews. It can be time-consuming going through resumes and cover letters, and you may be tempted to add more MAYBEs to the YES pile than necessary just to make sure you have options. Try to resist that urge.

Instead, follow up immediately with YES candidates, and keep applications rolling in so you can find even more of them. If you still aren't having any luck after several rounds of interviews, then it's time to review the MAYBE pile, but only then.

KEY TAKEAWAYS

- **Look for key elements.** *Make sure resumes and cover letters contain all of the necessary information and address your specific criteria, tailoring skills and experience to the job.*

- **Review resumes and cover letters in combination.** *They can work to reinforce, or undermine, a candidate's application.*

- **Call your YES applicants immediately.** *Don't let the most promising candidates get away by having them wait for you to complete the review process. Conduct preliminary interviews as soon as possible.*

CHAPTER 6

THE PHONE INTERVIEW

This is where the fun (or you might think, challenge) begins. You've narrowed your candidate list, and the next step is to arrange a series of interviews to see who can successfully cross the finish line. Each of these interviews (phone, in-person/virtual, working interview) provides an opportunity to get to know and assess the candidates and decide if you want to move them forward in your hiring process.

If you've done your job well by focusing on the position and the criteria candidates must meet to fill the open position, then the decisions should be fairly easy to make, and the list will naturally shorten until you have the strongest person at the end. Of course, you also may find you need to make adjustments along the way, and you should feel free to do so.

Be professional and transparent in all dealings with candidates. Make sure they know your hiring timeline and next steps. Don't string people along or "ghost" them by failing to notify them of rejection. And realize that you don't *have* to choose from any of these candidates if they do not meet your needs or if the person you want turns you down. While that is not something anyone relishes, you can always reboot the hiring process and start over again.

Every hire counts, particularly in a small business environment. Determination, not desperation, is the key when it comes to building your team for success.

REACH OUT

When you've found your YES candidates, the next step is to start making calls or sending emails to arrange phone interviews. Estimate how much time you think you'll need for each interview, and add a little extra in case you need it so that you won't be rushed off the phone in too much of a hurry to allow enough time to talk and to take notes. The phone interview is not only an important get-to-know-you step but your second important screening tool—one that can save you considerable time and energy.

If the phone interview is effective enough, you won't have to spend unnecessary time in a virtual or face-to-face interview. It's much easier to end a phone call in a matter of minutes. In a virtual or face-to-face interview, it is harder to cut the interview short after the person has spent the time coming to you or planning to meet with you; therefore, it takes more time.

A phone interview primarily allows you to do the following:

- **Get a first impression.** While you can't tell everything about someone over the phone, you can tell if they seem professional, articulate, and excited about your job opportunity. Unlike a large corporation, where candidates are often screened first by HR, you have the chance to get a firsthand impression of potential employees yourself.

- **Resolve any red flags or resume gaps.** By investigating any observations or concerns at this early stage, you can decide whether they are valid, and ensure that only quality candidates stay on your radar going forward.

PREPARE FOR THE INTERVIEW

Schedule phone interviews for when you can remain uninterrupted and focus your attention fully on the candidate. Don't talk to someone while you are trying to multitask or doing something else. You might think that you are saving yourself time, but in the long run, hiring the wrong candidate will cost you a lot more time, energy, and effort. You also risk leaving the candidate with a bad impression by sounding distracted or not paying attention to their comments and questions. Show respect for their time and effort as well.

I tend to be very good at multitasking, so talking on the phone while trying to manage an office, answer emails, and perform a myriad of other tasks is normal for me. I've conducted phone interviews while multitasking, however, and inevitably regretted it during the in-person interview as they rambled on and I realized I could have screened them better. (Note: Save Zoom or another video option for the second round of interviews, which will take longer.)

Before you make the call, make sure to have the candidate's resume in front of you. Annotate it so that you can remember the things you want to ask, and create a separate list of questions to check off. If you do this before you call, you'll know what to ask and run a smoother, more organized interview. If the items are not marked, there is a chance that you could get into a conversation with the candidate and forget to ask about your most important concerns.

At the same time, allow the conversation to take a natural course. You want to get a sense of what the candidate is really like, and sticking too closely to a question-and-answer format may not accomplish that. That is not to say you should let someone go on and on, but you can conduct an efficient and productive interview by striking a balance between a formal interview and an introductory conversation.

Be sure to ask the same questions of each candidate and prepare follow-up questions to dig deeper. Think about how you'll answer their questions as well. Try to be mindful of your tone and language, and evaluate theirs. Take careful notes, not only about their answers to your questions but about your general impressions. Is someone polite? Do they seem interested/interesting? Are they articulate (if that is needed in your vacant position)? Do their answers make sense and align with their resume and cover letter?

Know what is acceptable for a candidate to tell you and what is not. If you get the feeling someone is lying, then they probably are, and there's no good reason to stay on the phone any longer. If they are inappropriate or clearly lack the skills on their resume, then it's time to sign off, courteously. Let them know you won't be moving forward with their application and wish them the best of luck.

As a small business, your reputation is of utmost importance. You want to leave people with the feeling that they have been respected because you never know whom they will speak with or when you may cross paths again.

ARRANGE THE INTERVIEW

You won't always reach a candidate on your first try, and even if you don't, you may get enough information about them that you know to strike them off your list. You can call or email them to set up a time and date for the interview, and either way works.

I personally prefer calling someone and getting their voicemail first so that I can hear their message and see how long it will take them to call me back. This allows me to gauge their professionalism and how interested they are in the position.

To be honest, probably 30 percent of the time, I hang up without

64

leaving a message. Sometimes, it's because their voicemail is unprofessional or inappropriate. To put this into perspective, remember that this person knows they are looking for a job. They know that there will be potential employers calling them because they listed their phone number on their resume. If they haven't adjusted their message accordingly, then they aren't showing the awareness or careful attention I expect in an employee.

Many times, I call a candidate and hear, "Hey, if you get this message, I am probably out partying somewhere and can't hear my phone. You know what to do." Beep. Yes, I know what to do—move on to another candidate. In my view, if this person can't take the time to record a voicemail that at least wants to make me leave a message for them about a job opportunity, then I can tell they are not a good fit for my small business.

If a candidate's voicemail passes muster, I let them know that I am calling about the open position and state my name and phone number. I add that I'm actively looking for a great candidate and would like them to please call me back so we can discuss their resume. I always make sure to convey a little sense of urgency.

I also mark the time and date of my call on top of their resume so I know how long it takes them to call me back. I understand they may be working, but if they don't call back in the next couple of days, I consider that a red flag and may rule them out as a candidate. When they return my call, I'm also interested in whether they ask for me by name or tell the receptionist, "Someone called me about a job and I'm returning their call." I pay attention to their tone of voice and whether they are calling me from a quiet place or a noisy café, for instance. These attention-to-detail clues inform my decision-making about whether someone has good or bad judgment and would be an asset or a liability as an employee.

If someone answers the phone when I call them and they are whispering, I can usually tell it's because they are taking my call at work, and that's not acceptable to me. There's little chance I'll ask this person for an in-person interview if they knowingly take my call when they are on the job because it raises questions about their judgment and trustworthiness, both traits that are especially important in small business.

I always ask if this is a good time for them to talk for two reasons: First, because it is polite and a good way for them to tell me it is not and ask to call me back, and second, because I need them to make that decision.

I actually had one woman ask me to hold on for a minute while she stepped away from her desk. She went into the bathroom to continue the call with me, even as a coworker knocked on the door. The woman apologized that she needed to flush the toilet so that her coworker wouldn't suspect she was doing a job interview. I'm sorry, but there is no way that I am going to consider someone like that.

I understand job seekers might be excited about an interview, but I also want them to be able to use good judgment and consider their environment. For example, if a police officer is writing me a speeding ticket, would it be appropriate for me to ask them to hold on one second so I can take the call on my cell phone? Or if I was at the opera and my cell phone rang, would it make sense for me to answer the call?

If someone asks whether they can call me back at a convenient time, I try to tell if they are writing down my name and number. Do they confirm the time and date? Are they polite? Again, listen for these clues to predict how they might perform as a future employee.

The same assessment can be made about an email. Do they call or write you back? Does the email contain misspelled words or grammatical errors? Do they address you by the correct name and title? Does their message convey excitement and professionalism? Every bit of information helps.

CONDUCT THE INTERVIEW

As you begin your interview, it's a good idea to start with a polite greeting and some small talk to build rapport and make the candidate more comfortable. Pay attention to whether they greet you in a pleasant way, and see if you can tell whether your call is important to them.

Don't just listen for the words they say but also how they say them. You can gauge their confidence and professionalism by their tone of voice and their body language, which you can hear over the phone. Listen for things like yawns, if they are busy doing other things at the same time, or for smiling, which you can hear through a phone. The *way* someone answers a question can be just as important as *how* they answer.

For instance, if you ask someone how they handled a conflict with a customer or another coworker, you can tell if it went well or still bothers them just by listening to their tone and the way they respond. If they truly handled a conflict well, they will likely sound proud and open about the process, and you will hear it in their tone of voice. However, if the candidate feels they handled it well because they proved their point to the other person, you may hear more assertiveness or aggressiveness in their voice. You should evaluate not only the situation they are describing but their apparent feelings about the situation now.

I recommend using open-ended questions. At this stage, you are not trying to sell a candidate on your job but instead deciding whether you want to bring them in for a formal interview. Open-ended questions provide a way for candidates to communicate more expansively than merely answering yes or no, and that can give you a better sense of their personality.

Here are some examples:

- Tell me about yourself.

- Tell me about your current or last position.

- What are you looking for in your next position?

- What responsibilities do you have in your current role?

- Why are you looking for a new position?

You are listening not only for their response, which should validate the information you already have and provide some new insights, but also for the way they articulate the information. Can they answer a question with some detail but not too much? Do they know how to put a complete sentence together? Do they answer your question and not go off on a tangent? Do they go on and on and never really get to the point? The way they answer serves as a predictor of how they may be as an employee, as it reflects their communication skills and their ability to listen, analyze, and respond.

For example, if I ask candidates to tell me a bit about what they are looking for in a new position and they answer with a few things that seem positive and reasonable, I'm okay with that. However, I've gotten answers from one extreme to the other.

I had one candidate say they wanted a new job because they just got fired, while another one said, "I quit my job because I need to find one that pays better." I am not sure that I need to point this out to you, but these are *not* good answers. I've also had candidates go on and on long after I asked the question, rambling from one subject to another. This is also not a good sign and shows me they cannot communicate well or concisely organize their thoughts. I know this might not seem like much now, but when you ignore these signs and hire people like this, you end up with an employee who will either quit because they decide they want to get paid more or an employee who only wants to sit around and talk. Listening attentively is critical during this part of the hiring process.

Trust me, you don't want a new employee who takes ten minutes to give you a roundabout answer to every question. Nor do you want someone who cuts you off to tell you a story that is not relevant to the subject at hand.

While your conversation will vary from person to person, be sure you ask some basic questions of each and get the answers you need to decide whether to move the candidate forward. You can also establish two sets of questions so that if a candidate answers the first set poorly, you can end the conversation; if they answer well, you can continue the interview.

Here are some key questions to consider asking in your initial screening:

- How did you find out about this job?

- What do you know about our company?

- Tell me about yourself/walk me through your resume.

- Describe what you do now. Why do you want to leave?

- What interests you about this job?

- Do you have experience in [specific criteria for your job vacancy]?

- What would you say are your greatest strengths/weaknesses?

- When can you start?

- What are your salary requirements?

Important note: It's illegal in most states to ask about someone's current salary and salary history, and it's always prohibited to inquire about someone's race/ethnic identity, religion, gender identity, sexual orientation, marital status, pregnancy or family status, age, and disability or genetic information. Be sure to check your federal, state, and local employment laws and stay updated as they evolve. Also, take care not to ask questions that you may consider roundabout ways of discovering this information, such as "What neighborhood do you live in?"

- Do you have any questions for me? What else would you like me to know?

Be sure to address concerns related to a candidate's resume or cover letter, such as the following:

Employment gaps. Gaps may take the form of omissions, nonlinear employment, or short tenure. There are a number of reasonable explanations for them, which may already be addressed in a cover letter, and you have to determine whether a candidate's answer qualifies as reasonable while also ensuring that you comply with employment laws.

You can ask, "I see you did not work for this certain period of time. What can you tell me about that?" Listen closely to what the candidate says, and consider whether it suggests any problems with motivation, commitment, loyalty, or reliability.

If the reason had to do with career development or education, you can generally feel free to ask follow-up questions such as "What new skills did you acquire?" or "Why did you decide to do that?" A prepared candidate will offer a thoughtful and complete response.

If they blame a past employer or someone else for short job tenure, or if they repeatedly left jobs after a short time for bigger paychecks, then you might want to think twice about taking them on.

Personal reasons for employment gaps are trickier to address, and it's best for legal reasons to move on to another topic if the candidate's answer has to do with a family situation (having a baby, etc.) or health issue, for instance. However, at least you know that they had a valid reason for the gap, and it wasn't just because they could not find a job.

Location. If you're considering a candidate from another city/town or state, this is the time to ask about their willingness to relocate or deal with a long commute. The directness with which they answer the question, and the detail they provide, will tell you whether they have given it prior thought or if they are just waiting to see if they get the job before figuring it out. Winging it isn't good.

As a small business, you likely can't afford to subsidize someone's move or a long commute on top of their salary, unlike large corporations that can offer such benefits. It may also be important to you that they live in or near your community so they can be part of the local fabric.

I'm telling you this from experience and hope you can learn from my lessons. I once interviewed someone who told me that the commute was not going to be a big deal. It was forty-five minutes one way, and she told me she was confident she would have no problem, that she had done it before. This was during a time when unemployment was high and finding a new job was tough, so I thought she was being honest. However, when the economy turned around ten months later and businesses started hiring again, things changed. I had trained her for months, mind you, but she came to me at that point and told me her commute had become untenable.

Listen closely. You don't want to make an offer to a candidate only to have them withdraw because of the geographic distance.

MAKE SOME DECISIONS

Too many times, we're so desperate to fill an opening that we rationalize legitimate concerns or accommodate unsatisfying information. Don't. This is the time to focus on the people who are likely to be great employees. They are the ones worth taking the time and energy away from your work to interview in person. Don't waste your time trying to fit round pegs into square holes.

Even if you feel as if someone is a strong communicator, meets your skills criteria, and seems professional, you may have a negative gut feeling about them. Trust it and move on to the next candidate. This is not the time to find the perfect candidate, but it *is* the time to reject those who don't seem or feel right, especially since they will be working side by side with you and your team every day.

Once you've completed the first round of phone interviews, it's a good idea to sort candidates into the same three categories as before:

The YES pile. Let these candidates know at the end of your phone interview what your hiring timeline looks like and that you would like to schedule an in-person interview with them. Continue listening to their responses. Do they sound excited at the prospect of meeting you and your team? Are they motivated to find a day and time that works? Do they ask appropriate and relevant questions, such as "Should I bring anything with me?" or "What is the workplace dress code?" or "Should I call to confirm before the appointment?" It's also always nice if a candidate says they look forward to the opportunity.

I once had someone ask if it was okay to bring her baby to the interview, which I didn't find appropriate. I told her honestly that I preferred that she did not, and she kind of sighed and said she would see what she could do to find someone to watch the baby. After we hung up and I thought about it, I decided that I would interview her but would not hire her. If she was already having babysitting issues and making what I consider to be bad judgment calls, then she would probably not be a good fit for our office. Luckily, the next day she called to cancel the interview because she could not find childcare. She also said that her husband thought it might be too soon for her to consider a new job. I agreed with him. Her resume went into the NO pile.

The NO pile. Don't waste your time on candidates whose experience, personalities, skills, or interests do not fit your needs. Let them down lightly but directly. You can say, "I appreciate that you took the time to speak with me, but we've received many applications, and I think we're going to have to pass on yours now. I wish you all the best on your search." If the candidate asks why they are not moving forward, your explanation should be polite and fact-based (e.g., lack of skills, experience) versus subjective (e.g., personality, gut feeling).

If you hear something that gives you pause and makes you think that maybe they would be a good fit after all, note that on their resume and consider moving them to the MAYBE pile. Someone could wind up in the MAYBE pile because they are still in school and looking for a position after they graduate, but you need to hire now. You might want to consider them if you have not filled the position by that time or need to hire again in the future.

The MAYBE pile. These are the people who didn't impress you enough to merit an automatic in-person interview. My recommendation is to put these applications aside for now and come back to them later if you have additional openings or your first round of interviews fails to produce a winner. Let these candidates know your timeline and when they can expect to hear if you are going to move forward with their application. Be sure to note those dates on your own calendar so you can get back to them when you said you would.

And again, listen to how they respond. Are they upbeat and looking forward to hearing from you? Or do they thank you and hang up? Write down some notes in the moment about your decision so you can refer to them later.

It's possible they were having a bad day, and when they realized you were about to end the call, they realized they had to step up. That's fine, but it's also unlikely. Thank them for their time and tell them you will be back in touch if things change—but move on. And if they just hang up, then you know you made the right decision.

Honestly, having these resumes on hold is more for you to feel better about not tossing them into the trash or the NO pile than for them to actually get another interview. It may help you feel more optimistic about your search if you feel you have a full bench of candidates moving forward, and even if I tell you to throw these resumes out, I know you probably won't. No one likes to reject people. But in the end, you will likely regret hiring one of these candidates because they don't work out for the very reasons you resisted hiring them at first. I know, because I've done it.

I've actually done it more times than I care to admit, but I think we're all tempted to lower our standards, subconsciously or not, when we're desperate to make a hire. One candidate who comes to mind seemed perfect, with all the right skills. She wasn't super impressive on the phone, and her interview was fair, but I really needed to fill the position. In my mind, I think I played up her skills as a higher priority and ignored the things about her that didn't thrill me.

Well, I hired her, and it was bad from the start. Everything I had not been happy about during the interview became apparent from the very first day. She worked for me for about two weeks, and those were probably the longest two weeks of my life. I really hoped she would work out, and I hated to be wrong. At the end of two weeks, I let her go and was relieved that I no longer had to work with her, but she had already made friends with some of my employees, and they hang out still today. I see her in photos with my team on social media, and it's a reminder to me to trust my gut. There's a reason some candidates land in the MAYBE pile.

Throughout this part of the process, continue to reach out to people with promising experience. It may help to schedule a designated time each day to review new resumes and arrange more interviews. Until you've extended an offer, keep your options open and those potential hires rolling in.

KEY TAKEAWAYS

- **Arrange phone interviews to get first impressions and address red flags.** *Use this early-stage screening tool to figure out who should move ahead in your hiring process.*

- **Pay close attention.** *Everything from a person's voicemail message to how they answer questions gives you the information you need to evaluate their application.*

- **Make sure you get the information you need.** *Prepare a list of questions and follow-ups so you don't forget to ask important questions or address concerns.*

CHAPTER 7

THE FORMAL INTERVIEW

Most people hiring for a position probably start with the face-to-face or virtual interview, but I believe you should prepare up front to set yourself up for success. You can look forward to meeting the candidates in person (or via Zoom or another video option) because you have already reviewed their resumes, have had productive conversations, and like them enough to bring them in.

If we've learned anything from the COVID-19 pandemic and the potential for any future shelter-in-place or quarantine orders, many small businesses have had to shift to remote interviews, even virtual onboarding, without ever meeting candidates in person. All of my team members at Front Office Rocks are virtual, and I still have not met two of them in person. We have an awesome team that is very productive and connected across the country.

If you use Zoom or other video software to conduct interviews, be sure the technology works properly so you don't have any issues during the interview process. Try to use a headset instead of the speakerphone for clarity and sound control. Don't expect a candidate to turn on their video if you don't, and vice versa. It's only fair, and fairness is an important aspect of the employer-employee relationship.

You may be disappointed that you can't assess someone face-to-face, but there are advantages. Scheduling may be more flexible and convenient for candidates. They also may be more comfortable in their own environment, and you'll still be able to evaluate their communication skills, such as eye contact and body language.

PREPARE FOR THE INTERVIEW

Remember that a candidate may look good on a resume or sound promising on the phone, but this second-stage interview is the real deal, and it's important that you have your act together as much as you expect your new hire to. But it's also a time to get excited as well: You're one step closer to finding the next star employee for your team.

First, be sure to dress and act professionally for the occasion and choose a professional setting. Candidates will be interested to see what your small business office looks like. If you use Zoom or another video conferencing program, dress the same way you would as if you were conducting an in-person interview.

Second, schedule virtual and face-to-face interviews with sufficient time. Just as there isn't a one-size-fits-all approach to interviewing, I'd say there isn't a specific amount of time that works for all jobs and all candidates. I've had interviews last as little as ten minutes because I knew from the moment a candidate walked in that they weren't going to be a fit. I've also had interviews that exceeded an hour because I knew these were people I wanted to hire, or it took me longer to decide if they were a good fit or not.

Certain situations may require longer interviews. You may have technical requirements for particular jobs, or people on your team may also need to interview the candidate to assess their skills and qualifications. Consider online scheduling and tracking apps to manage interviews and staff availability.

Remember that the candidate took the time to meet with you. Allow enough time to make sure they feel heard and you had a good chance to make your decision. At the same time, you can feel free to cut an interview short if it is clearly going nowhere. Too many times, interviews can drag on and waste time in which you could be doing something more productive. Be in control of the interview, so it lasts as long as you need it to in order to make the right decision. A typical interview might take anywhere from thirty minutes to an hour or more for an especially serious candidate.

Third, it's important to focus. We all get busy, but if you're distracted and trying to squeeze in an interview between other tasks, you'll miss a lot of important information that could result in a bad hire. You also risk giving the wrong impression to your candidate. Don't rush or appear frazzled. Especially with a small business, you want to convey that you know what you're doing and that you run an organized enterprise with a positive environment. That may mean rescheduling if something important comes up, or conducting the interview somewhere off-site, where you won't be distracted or interrupted.

Do everything you can to ensure that you can be fully present and conduct the most productive interview possible.

TIP: SCHEDULE MULTIPLE INTERVIEWS CLOSE TOGETHER

If you intend to interview multiple candidates, it's a good idea to schedule the interviews relatively close to one another instead of days or weeks apart. Establish a timeline, and schedule consecutive interviews as soon as possible.

The advantage is that you can more easily compare candidates because they are fresh in your mind. This can help you make decisions and more quickly find a good hire.

continued

If you spread interviews too far apart, it's easy to forget details about people, especially the ones with whom you spoke early on. In addition, you risk losing good candidates to other employers by making them wait too long to meet with you.

REVIEW CANDIDATE MATERIALS

Prior to the interview, make sure you have everything in order. Prepare your thoughts, questions, and materials so you're ready and know exactly to whom you'll be speaking. This means reviewing your short list of interviewees, looking over their resumes and application materials, and thinking about what stood out to you as well as any red flags.

It's also a good time to return to your original criteria for the job. It's easy to forget about those requirements in the shuffle of scheduling interviews and other logistics. The danger is that we may not realize until it's too late that we've selected a candidate who fails to check most of the boxes. Keeping what you want and need at the top of your mind, even with adjustments, will guide you during the interview and question-and-answer process.

EXTEND INVITATIONS

The number of candidates to invite for a virtual or in-person interview varies, depending on the job, the market, and the candidates. It depends first on how difficult you think it might be to fill the position. In a tight job market, businesses have a harder time finding qualified candidates, but when we face high unemployment or significant small business closures, there's likely to be a much larger pool from which to choose.

Of course, we experienced and can learn from the exceptional times in 2020 with COVID-19: A Facebook survey of 86,000 small and medium-sized businesses (which tend to be younger than large businesses) showed that of the businesses forced to shut down during the pandemic, more than half said they wouldn't rehire the same workers they had before the crisis.[1] And unemployment reached record levels, putting more pressure on small businesses to screen candidates and hire and retain good workers who could help them thrive and survive in volatile times.

Skills are another factor in deciding how many people to invite for second interviews. If you have a very technical position, particularly one that requires certification or training, I would bring in every YES candidate. Conversely, you might want to bring in only the top candidates for an entry- or lower-level role that will be relatively easy to fill.

For instance, if you have time to do ten interviews for a lower-level position and you have twenty YES candidates, then I would bring in the top ten. If you still don't find the right candidate, then you can bring in the others.

CHOOSE THE TYPE OF INTERVIEW

If you have a large number of promising candidates, you might consider whether you want to conduct in-person or virtual interviews by yourself or involve one or more trusted people on your team to participate or interview the candidates themselves.

There's no one "right" way. Remember, all you want to do is find out if each candidate is a potential hire or not. Here are the primary interview options:

One-on-one interview. You can conduct some or all of the interviews, or you could ask someone on your team to do the first interviews and give you their feedback and recommendations. In effect, they would provide additional screening and might appreciate the opportunity to be part of your decision-making process. Make sure they have a complete list of questions and are clear about your hiring criteria.

Group interview. If you have twenty or thirty people interviewing for a receptionist position, you or your team could convene a group session with multiple candidates to tell them a little bit about your business and complete a skills assessment to help you narrow the field. Skills assessments can include a test or a case study to evaluate.

Not all candidates will like this approach, however, because it gives them less opportunity to differentiate themselves and impress you. It can be stressful and time-consuming for potential employees, so be sure to allot sufficient time and allow for breaks. Also make sure that anyone who participates in the interview process understands the legal restrictions with interview questions.

Panel interview. If you have a particularly busy schedule, it might be a good idea to have a few individuals on your team conduct individual interviews together or one right after the other. Delegating this job gives your team an opportunity to provide input, and it saves you time. Also, if the role is a highly technical position, you may need the assessment of a team member who has or is familiar with the applicable skills. Or if the new hire will be working one-on-one with a particular team member, you may want to gauge compatibility.

Similar to a skills assessment given during a group interview, you might ask a candidate to complete a short coding project or outline a social media strategy. You can also use specific skills exams during the hiring process, and it's always a good idea to compensate candidates for their time, especially if they are asked to complete these types of assessments on their own time.

Off-site interviews. Other types of interviews include coffee or lunch interviews outside the office, which provide a more casual environment for prospective employees. Make sure you choose a quiet, convenient location that allows for some privacy to conduct the interview. And yes, you are expected to pay for the coffee or lunch if you extended the invitation.

WHAT TO LOOK FOR

The phone interview not only sifts out unqualified candidates but also gives you confidence in your ability to find the right person, possibly making the process more enjoyable. The in-person or video interview involves a more in-depth assessment of how the candidate communicates and whether they understand your company and what it does. You also can evaluate whether they possess the soft skills needed to work with your team, as well as the hard skills that they have acquired or can be taught. It's also an opportunity to "sell" your position and business to them.

Here are three *P*'s for you and your team to consider:

Professionalism. Do they arrive early or on time to your interview, whether in-person or virtual? Or do they arrive late? Are they dressed appropriately for an interview and for your particular industry? Or does it look as though they just rolled out of bed? This isn't about whether they are wearing expensive designer labels or are physically attractive. This is about understanding the environment and showing respect. You wouldn't necessarily expect someone interviewing for a line cook position to wear a suit and tie, for instance.

In the dental field, I see this all the time with people who are accustomed to wearing scrubs. I speak at dental conferences around the country, where participants attend often on weekends for a full day or multiple days. Inevitably, there are people in the audience wearing scrubs. I always wonder what they're thinking. Are they expecting a dental emergency to happen at any minute, and they want to be prepared? Do they no longer have any other clothes? It never makes sense to me.

The point is the same thing happens in job interviews at dental offices all the time. Candidates arrive for their interview to be an office manager, a patient-facing management position, and they are wearing old, wrinkled scrubs. I understand that they might have come from their job or the scrubs are more comfortable, but they could have changed before they met with me. It's hard to think of them as professionals in my office when they dress for the interview that way.

Preparation. Does the candidate bring a copy of their resume, a portfolio, any professional licenses or certifications, or any other requested materials? Or are they just holding their cell phone or car keys? Do they turn off their cell phone? Do they take notes? Do they have references assembled for you? Or do they say they need to get back to you on that? They knew they were coming for a job interview, right? Take all of this into account.

Personality. Are they friendly? Do they smile? Or do they complain about bad traffic and take a seat before you invite them to sit down? Is this someone who would be interacting with your team and your customers, or would they be back-end support and not client-facing, and how does that align with their personality? Are they polite to your receptionist and other staff? Do they listen attentively and ask thoughtful questions? What does their body language say about how interested they are in the position and what you say?

I hear stories all the time from employers complaining about team members who show up late to work on a regular basis or come to work dressed unprofessionally. I ask them to tell me about their interview with that person. Nine times out of ten, they kind of laugh and say that the same thing happened at the interview. The employee was late or showed up disheveled or not dressed appropriately. This interview is like a book cover. You can't judge someone by it entirely, but it gives you a hint of what is to come.

CONDUCT THE INTERVIEW

I always start off with a polite greeting such as "Thanks for coming. It's nice to meet you." You can also say something like "I appreciate your taking the time to meet with us. Did you have any trouble finding us?" I want to see how they respond before we actually sit down and start the questions. I gauge their attitude and communication skills and evaluate the first impression they would make on my customers. Then I launch into a few open-ended questions to get the conversation rolling, just as I do on phone interviews.

You can open with a comment like, "We've talked on the phone. I know a little bit about your background, based on that call, but can you refresh my memory?" Give candidates a while to talk, and consider whether they ramble and seem uncomfortable or offer an articulate and organized explanation of their background and experience. Perhaps they wrap up their answer in a minute. Have you gotten what you need to know, in the way you want to know?

Don't hurry to fill any silence. Sometimes, the best information flows from unanticipated moments, and good communication skills can be one of the hardest things to find in an employee. This is a key point. Too many of us listen with the intention of what we are going to say next. Make sure during these interviews that you are actively and not passively listening. At this point of the interview, you're not trying to sell them on you but trying to learn more about them. If you are nervous or always find yourself filling in whenever there is silence, try to change that habit.

Once you've set the tone, and the candidate seems as comfortable as they are going to be, you can start asking concrete questions about their experience and skills. This is the time to discreetly run down your checklist.

If I know immediately that this is not the right candidate for my business, or for any position, then I may ask one or two questions based on their resume just to double-check there's nothing I'm missing. After all, they passed the first screening. If additional questions don't produce any positive information, I may end the interview there. But if I'm getting a good feeling again, then it's time to dig in.

I start by asking about specific jobs and places they've worked. I want to know about their responsibilities, accomplishments, and impact. Did they help grow the company? Did they move up the ladder? Did they take on more responsibility? Did they receive any special training?

I want to know about experiences and skills that translate to my business, including some I may not have even considered. I'm constantly taking notes and checking that what they tell me aligns with their resume. Ultimately, I'm constantly wondering this: Are we a match?

Here are some great examples of interview questions that can be adapted to your particular industry and available position:

- **Tell me about your best supervisor and your worst supervisor. What did you like/dislike about them?** I want to hear if the candidates offer objective assessments or try to shift blame for poor performance/reviews. I also want to know if the traits they like/dislike align with my business and team.

- **Tell me about a project or job where you helped improve a business or some aspect of a business.** I want to hear how they discuss their accomplishments. It doesn't matter if they were on a team to get their project accomplished. I just want to know how they contributed to the business goals above and beyond what their previous jobs specifically entailed.

- **Tell me about a time you had a conflict with another employee or customer and how you handled it.** I listen for problem-solving abilities and professionalism. Did they escalate a problem, or did they know how to creatively solve it?

- **If I were to ask your coworkers what it's like to work with you, what would they say?** By asking them about what a coworker would say, they don't have to brag but can still offer some positive (hopefully honest) reflections about themselves and perhaps provide some insights into areas they could improve.

- **What is your best trait and where do you think you could improve?** Most candidates don't want to share anything negative about themselves, but if they are prepared for this question, then they should be able to offer a constructive critique that shows self-awareness and acknowledges room for growth.

- **Why should we hire you?** By this point, I'm looking for a strong, confident, thoughtful answer. They should be able to sell themselves to me.

I also want to be sure to address any red flags on their resumes. If they had a lot of jobs, I ask why. I want to understand employment gaps and observe their verbal and nonverbal cues for signs that they are confident and truthful. I'm listening for potential problems and weighing their answers against my needs. If they say they left jobs where they were not given enough autonomy, then that might work well in a business that thrives on worker independence, but it won't work in a business that requires intense collaboration and teamwork. If your position is client-facing, then it's important to know if they like working with people or prefer back-end support.

Did they leave previous jobs for more money, a shorter commute, or lack of upward mobility? Past experience can dictate future performance, and small businesses often cannot provide the salary levels or opportunities for career advancement that some candidates seek.

In terms of finding out about specific hard or technical skills, I suggest presenting candidates with opportunities to tell stories about how they applied their skills rather than giving them yes-or-no questions. For instance, you can say, "Tell me about a time when you used [a skill] to [provide a solution]." You want concrete examples in context so that you can truly assess if they have the hands-on experience you need or if they are willing to learn, and if they are willing and able to jump into any number of demanding situations that most small businesses require.

I also weave in questions that are more personality or soft-skill-based, such as "What do you think is your greatest strength, and where do you think you have room to grow?" Interestingly, sometimes the answer may seem like a positive to them, but it's a negative for you. For example, they might tell you that they want to get their job done and impress their boss, so they don't have a lot of time for their colleagues. They may think they sound focused and ambitious, but you may be looking for more of a team player who enjoys collaborating.

I once had a candidate tell me her greatest strength was being a "people person," so the thing she needed to work on the most was her failure to get her job done because she spent so much time communicating with her coworkers. Another candidate explained that his biggest challenge was anger management when others did not commit to getting the job done as he did. He was proud he was doing better, but when others didn't keep up with him, he could get mad. Thankfully, I never witnessed either of these candidates in action because I did not hire them.

I also ask things like, "Tell me about a time when you had to deal with somebody who was difficult, a colleague or client, and you were getting some pushback." Give them some conflict or problem-solving questions to see how they handle conflict resolution and troubleshooting. I sometimes ask to hear about their best and worst supervisors and why they felt that way about them. If they didn't like someone who expected them to meet deadlines, we probably have a problem! There are legitimate reasons for being unhappy at work, and then there are excuses.

Also, if you're interviewing people for a job that can be done remotely, you want to gauge how a candidate will perform from home. Here are some questions to ask about this situation:

- Have you previously worked remotely?

- What are the advantages/disadvantages of remote work?

- How is your home office set up?

- How do you schedule your day?

- What are your favorite time management tools?

- How do you stay motivated?

- How often do you check in with the main office?

- Do you work better alone or with a team?

- Would you be willing to come into the office from time to time?

Candidates also need to know about you, your business, the position, and what would be expected of them. They are interviewing you as much as you are interviewing them. Depending on how the interview is going, and particularly if you're not planning to hire the candidate, you can give a quick overview of the position and company to save time. However, if the candidate is a great fit, then you should spend more time here really explaining and highlighting the position, the company, and all of the other great things to sell them on wanting to work there. This typically falls near the end of the interview, once you have made up your mind on whether they are a potential new hire or not. Things you can discuss include what makes your company a great place to work, what you do differently and better, what the culture and team are like, and how you would describe your leadership style or that of the person they would be reporting to. Cite examples and let them know about your successes and potential for growth.

It's also important to ask candidates if they have any questions of their own, which is a great indicator of interest and enthusiasm. Specific questions about business growth, vacation time, company culture, and customers show more interest in the position than broader questions about company size or when it was founded.

Be enthusiastic yourself. For instance, provide detailed information about benefits to the top candidates and even those you are uncertain about. You want the best candidates to think, "I need to work here!"

KNOW HOW TO WRAP IT UP

Even before you begin an interview, you need a plan for after the interview ends. Do you intend to offer the best candidate a job on the spot (not generally recommended)? Or are you going to share the timeline for your hiring process?

You've likely identified your top contenders based on the interview time alone. Qualified candidates will take more of your time because you probably enjoy their company and want to know more. Candidates who aren't a right fit for your small business likely didn't pass muster due to a lack of hard skills or soft skill deficiencies. Those in between may be worth another look, depending on how many people you have decided to move forward in the process.

It's critical to be transparent with the timeline and process, letting candidates know when they can expect to hear from you and thanking them for their time. Check in with them, too, if your time-line changes. You'll also want to let them know if you'll be checking their references and if there are other background checks or drug tests involved in being hired.

Let top candidates know if you want them to conduct a second interview with other team members and that you'll be in touch to get them scheduled. Asking about their availability is another good way to gauge their interest and to elicit information about whether they are considering other offers.

The way they leave the interview—polite and excited or gloomy and abrupt—can also tell you something about who they are and whether they are a fit for your team. Regardless, you want any candidate who interviews with your business to leave feeling good about the experience. Word travels fast, especially if you're a local enterprise, and a bad impression can hurt your business and put off others from applying.

Be sure to take notes immediately on their resumes to keep the information in one place and flag any outstanding concerns. It might even help to develop a rating system so you can quickly prioritize who to interview first to reduce the risk of their taking another job.

Do a gut check, too. How did that person make you feel? Respected and listened to? Or distracted and neutral? Is this someone you want to work with day to day? How will your customers respond? Will they get along with your team? Most small businesses don't fire employees because they lacked particular hard skills. They fire them due to softer skills such as communication and personality issues—for example, not showing up to work on time or causing too much drama. If you suspect this could be a problem, then move on.

I once had an employee who didn't get along with others. She was good at her job, but she never smiled or tried to appear pleasant or happy. I noticed this in the interview but assumed it was because she was nervous. Well, that was not the case.

After I hired her, she walked around with a permanent scowl on her face, and people thought she was mad. Patients complained she was not friendly, and team members kept coming to me to tell me that she had an attitude or seemed to have an issue all the time. I counseled her multiple times, but she never got better or even showed any sign of trying. It translated into her not being considered a team player and caused drama in the office. She didn't want to try to improve her attitude and, in fact, got worse until I finally had to let her go.

Even if you have made a decision one way or another, remember that even during this part of the interview process, you are still being evaluated. You might have decided that they are a good fit, but they might not have made up their mind about you. Qualified candidates are going to be cautious about leaving their current job or making a wrong move.

When it comes to interviews, everyone has to put their best foot forward the entire time and even with any follow-up communication or next steps.

KEY TAKEAWAYS

- Use face-to-face or virtual interviews to explore top candidates' soft and hard skills in-depth. *Plan the type of interview that is appropriate for the position, and review materials in advance.*

- Look for the three *P*'s: professionalism, preparation, and personality. *Pay attention to signals that show whether someone has done their homework, can work well with your team, and has the hands-on experience to get the job done.*

- **Combine open-ended questions with specific questions to elicit a range of responses.** *Find out if candidates can sell themselves to you in informed, articulate, and organized ways in an interview that feels more like a conversation.*

CHAPTER 8

THE WORKING INTERVIEW

You'll never really know if you've found the right candidate until they start working for you. Like first dates, many people look and say the right things during the interview process, and it's only after they've been hired that they begin to let their guard down and reveal their true selves.

Some of the best hiring decisions I've made were largely based on seeing people in our work environment. For instance, I had an interview with a woman who insisted over and over again that she was a team player. She repeatedly emphasized that she led by example and felt that everyone should pull their weight to get a job done.

I loved that attitude and invited her to come spend the day with us. She seemed to do a good job that day and do what was asked of her. Nothing stood out to me until the end of the day when I sat down with her to see whether she liked the office and how her day went. She told me that the day went well but she just had one question. She was asked twice to sweep and wanted to know when the other team members would take their turns sweeping, too. She didn't find it fair that she swept twice and one of the other team members did not sweep at all, a comment that obviously ran counter to what she had told me about herself in the interview.

The stakes are high for small business hires. We have to do more with fewer people and require those people to be reliable and on task. High turnover is particularly problematic for small start-ups and can be expensive—in 2018, the average company spent around $4,000 and took twenty-four days to hire a new employee, according to Bersin by Deloitte.[1]

In the best-case scenario, you find out that you've made the right decision in employing someone. In the worst case, you realize you've made a mistake and have to let them go. For a small business, that can be not only inconvenient but costly, potentially affecting team morale, productivity, and culture, as well as your bottom line.

One of the best ways to put the odds in your favor is to invite one or two of your top candidates to participate in a tryout, or "working interview," where they spend a day on the job with you and your team. Of course, they won't tackle the full gamut of job responsibilities, but you can give them some actual tasks and see firsthand how they are likely to do in your office. You can also evaluate how they interact with coworkers and clients. By the same token, it allows the candidate to get a better sense of your business, the work environment, and the culture.

A working interview is not the time for you to spend additional hours with the candidate learning about their resume or sharing more about your company or the position with them; that should have been accomplished in the virtual or face-to-face interview. It's also not a time to start formally training the candidate for the position. Save that for if or when they are hired.

Finally, the working interview is not a time for your team to hang out and get to know the candidate, though that will happen a bit. It's a time for everyone to work and to see how the candidate performs.

PREPARE FOR THE WORKING INTERVIEW

Some candidates may not be familiar with the concept of a working interview, so it's important to set expectations and goals. I also recommend compensating candidates for their time (and in most cases, it is the law), especially since they may have to take a day off their current job to participate in your working interview. Even if payment is mandated by law, depending on the location of your business, it also sends the message that you are fair and respect your employees, which makes working for you more appealing. (Note: Some employment contracts may prohibit a candidate from taking contract work, and they may not want or be able to take a day off from their job. It's up to you to decide if a working interview is necessary for your opening.)

Small businesses also generally can't compete with the largesse of big companies, such as 401(k)s or lunch buffets, but they often can provide the kinds of advantages—fairness, work-life flexibility, close relationships, and respect—that make a real difference to job seekers. Bringing candidates into your environment is your opportunity to highlight what you offer.

When you explain the working interview to candidates, you want to give them general guidelines but also the latitude to act how they would typically act. (This is part of the test, right?) If they ask when to arrive, what to wear, whether they need to bring any supplies, or to whom they should report, that gives you a sense that they are going to start out on the right foot and are focused on the work. But if they ask what they should bring for lunch, if they can keep their cell phones with them, or how long they can take breaks, it might raise a red flag.

Make sure you know local, state, and federal employment laws and HR guidelines and ask candidates to sign relevant documents when they come in for the time in your office. You can find most of this information online, but you will want to consult an HR specialist or a lawyer if you are not clear about your state laws. In particular, you want to make sure that you have the right documentation confirming that this is a one-time arrangement that does not guarantee them a position and does not make them eligible for unemployment. You also want to make sure that you agreed on a payment rate with the candidate in advance.

It may seem a bit extreme to be so wary of your candidate, but I hear all the time about businesses getting burned. I know of a couple of dental offices where the candidate tried to file for unemployment after they spent a day in the working interview. Even though the dental office won in court, they still had to pay to fight the claim. It's always smart to protect your business, especially when dealing with people whom you don't know well.

PLAN THE DAY

Next, it's time to arrange some tasks for the candidate that will allow you to evaluate their performance. Here are some basic guidelines:

- **Avoid client-facing tasks.** You don't want to jeopardize your existing and potential customer relationships in case a candidate provides a bad experience or interaction. For instance, I would not recommend having candidates answer phones, since that is often the first client contact with your business. You might, however, have them sit at the front desk and greet people as they come in. That way, you can assess their customer service skills, but one of your regular employees can intervene if the situation starts to go south.

- **Avoid tasks that could potentially harm a client or patient.** For instance, you wouldn't want a candidate to provide legal or medical services, which could compromise or hurt a customer. I would never ask a candidate to provide dental services such as a cleaning or extraction in our office, for instance. Instead, you can ask them to support you or your team in providing services in ways that do not give them full responsibility for the task.

- **Choose tasks with measurable outcomes.** The type of tasks that you select for candidates should help you evaluate if they can do what they said they could in their interview and how they do it. The tasks should also show they understand the position that is available. For example, if they said they are good at completing things without needing a lot of direction, give them a task for which some people might need guidance. How do they make decisions? Can they figure things out on their own? Do they work too quickly or too slowly? Just as important, do they know when it is time to stop and ask for assistance?

- Of course, you want to give candidates a little slack because they are new, don't know your business well, and probably are a bit nervous. But if something should take only an hour and they need four hours to finish, then that's a red flag. Give them enough direction but not so much that you are doing it for them. Consider whether they ask the right questions, enough questions, or too many questions, or if they seem overwhelmed and don't ask you anything.

- **Choose tasks that are challenging but not absolutely necessary to the operation of your business that day.** Of course, it would be great to have them do something that you really need done, but you don't want to risk anything going seriously wrong. For example, you might have them alphabetize files (as long as they do not contain confidential information), call clients to confirm appointments, or update spreadsheets with information—a task that is not critical but would be nice if it got done. The idea here is to allow you to assess their skills without compromising your business in any way.

- **Include working sessions with team members.** This is a way to realistically see how the candidate communicates and functions in a collaborative setting. You may also want to test their skills with a particular software product or project management tool.

- **Be creative with remote work.** If your candidate will be working virtually, set up some tasks with deadlines that need to be done independently and also with team members. Consider giving them a project that requires presenting some information so you can gauge their communication and organization skills.

ARRANGE A DESIGNATED WORKSPACE

The tryout is also designed to see how candidates fit into your environment. You want to put them in a location close to where they would spend the majority of their time and the employees with whom they would be working. Don't stick them on a project in the stockroom, where they won't interact with anyone—unless that is going to be their job and you want to ensure they can work alone.

In most cases, you want to locate candidates close enough to other team members to allow for interaction but not interfere with your employees being attentive to their jobs. You also want to schedule time for breaks to give the candidate a rest and to provide for more casual interactions.

Consider the following: Do the candidates seem organized? Do they stay contained to their space or spread out? Do they respect other people's boundaries? Are they focused? Do they wander away from their designated area and around the office? Do they make too much small talk?

I remember a candidate who did a working interview for an IT position at a large law firm. The firm called after lunch and said that he was not going to work out. They sent him home without even finishing the day out, so I naturally wanted to know why. Apparently, the candidate spent the majority of the day in the restroom, at the water cooler, and talking to people as he walked by their cubicles. They said he was friendly but apparently *too* friendly and must have eaten something bad to have to use the restroom as much as he did. The funny thing is when I followed up with the candidate, he told me that the people at the law firm were all super nice and that they had amazing "facilities."

Some people constantly distract others, or they are distracted themselves. It's important to know this in advance, especially in a small business where space may be limited, and sound carries easily from one spot to another.

Another reason you should put candidates near your team members is so they can interact with each other, and you can get feedback from your employees. If the team works remotely, then make sure to schedule some virtual meeting interactions. There's a fine balance between healthy social interactions and all-day gossiping, and this provides a chance for you and your team to see where this candidate falls on that spectrum.

ENGAGE YOUR EMPLOYEES

It's important to let your team know that you'll be bringing candidates in for tryouts and what to expect. Encourage them to provide you with feedback based on their observations and interactions, to alert you immediately to any concerns or bad behavior, and to make sure they know that their opinions matter.

Take time to explain that you expect them to be polite and friendly but that you want work to proceed as usual and the candidate will be assigned tasks to complete. Team members can assist to a limited degree but should not interfere with your ability to see if the candidate can tackle the work, troubleshoot, follow directions, and get the job done.

OBSERVE THE CANDIDATE

With expectations set and arrangements made, it's time to see if you honestly think this candidate is a good fit. It can be hard sometimes because you want them to succeed and you're eager to make a hire. However, be careful not to overlook, justify, or ignore anything during the office tryout, because if you end up rushing to hire the candidate instead of taking your time to objectively rate their performance, it will come back to haunt you later. I guarantee it.

Here are some things to look for:

- Do they show up on time?

- Do they dress appropriately for the work environment?

- Are they friendly, respectful, and professional with you, your employees, and clients?

- Do they show up with the right attitude and ready to work?

- Do they follow directions and ask reasonable questions?

- Do they complete the assigned tasks? Could any mistakes be easily fixed with some training?

- Do they meet deadlines?

- Are they compatible with your team? Ask employees what they think about the candidate's work performance, communication, and social skills.

- Do they fit in with your business culture and seem aligned with your mission?

- At the end of the day, what did they do well and what did they do poorly?

- How did you feel about having the candidate in your office? Is this someone who can do the job well, fit into the organization, succeed with your customers, and be an asset to the team? What does your gut say?

As busy as you might be with your everyday work, make sure to slow down when you observe the candidates. Or, if you have someone on the team responsible for this person, make sure they know what to look for and report back to you. Also, check in with candidates throughout the day to see how they are doing. If they come to you with questions or suggestions, listen closely to their language and tone.

CONSIDER NEXT STEPS

Once you've evaluated the candidate's performance, spoken to your employees, and asked the candidate about their experience, it's time to consider whether you want to move forward with this person.

If you happen to know within the first few hours that they are not going to work out, which happens more often than not, there's no reason to keep them around as long as you planned. It's okay to pull them aside partway through the day to let them know they are no longer needed in the office, your plans have changed, and you appreciate their time.

You can let them know when you'll be back in touch with them, and be sure to deliver a timely and polite rejection when that time comes. There's probably a good chance they share your sense that things aren't working out, and you don't need more distractions in your office.

On the other hand, if a candidate seems to be working out, make sure you are making full use of the time to evaluate them. Leave time at the end of the day to find out how they feel about their work experience and if they have any questions. You might not be ready to pull the trigger and make a decision during or immediately after the tryout, and that's okay. Thank them for their time and explain the next steps in the hiring process. You might even feel confident enough to tell them that if everything checks out—references, background check—then they can expect an offer within a certain timeframe. You can also ask them to notify you if they receive any other job offers between now and then.

The one thing I can tell you is that if you feel strongly positive about a candidate, then that is typically a great sign. And if you feel overwhelmingly negative about a person, trust your instincts. You just saved yourself and your business a lot of headache—and money. If you're on the fence—maybe it's about the candidate or maybe you're overthinking the hire—then that's a good time to check in with your employees and any other observers.

A well-crafted day should help solidify your hiring decision, one way or the other, and save you time, money, and stress by avoiding disappointment later.

KEY TAKEAWAYS

- **Plan an effective tryout strategy in advance.** *Assign tasks that are measurable and provide opportunities for interaction and collaboration with you and your team. Avoid assigning tasks to a candidate that are client-facing and could potentially harm your business. Find ways to test skills, both hard and soft.*

- **Observe, observe, observe.** *Keep a close eye on the candidate throughout the day, stopping to check in with them, or assign someone on your team to keep watch and report back to you. Adjust tasks as needed so that you can find out what you need to know.*

- **Gather information.** *Assess what you've learned about the candidate, and consult with your team and any other observers to decide if you want to take the next step with their application. Trust your instincts and don't hesitate to cut a tryout short if it is not working out. Let promising candidates know what to expect next and when.*

CHAPTER 9

DIGGING DEEPER

This would not be a true hiring book without discussing the additional tools that many employers use to help determine if they have the right candidate for their position and to protect their small businesses, employees, and clients.

Small businesses often do not have an HR or legal department to handle this aspect of the hiring process. Because laws vary, it's best to consult an independent HR professional or legal advisor about what kind of employee research will work best for your business and to make sure you comply with local, state, and federal regulations.

Taking the time to check references and run a background check adds to the process, but it might be worth it to ensure you are making a good hire. According to a Monster.com survey, about three in four small business owners who have hired the wrong person before felt frustrated (73 percent), stressed (47 percent), and discouraged (36 percent) afterward. The survey also found that more than half of those who hired the wrong person experienced a loss of time (69 percent), money (56 percent), and customers (24 percent), as well as product errors (51 percent).[1]

Small business owners often overlook these additional checks, or safeguards, which can come back to burn them later. Embezzlement is an especially big problem in the dental industry, but it could be avoided if we all did background or reference checks.

Without safeguards like these, there is a significantly higher chance for things to happen, such as embezzlement. For example: A person works for a small company for a very long time and ends up being fired once it's discovered they have stolen money or other things from the company. Understandably, the small business owner is embarrassed and might not even want to press charges, and the employee goes on to look for a new job, lying to prospective new employers about their work history and falsifying the reason for their departure.

There's no way to find out the truth without checking references or doing a background check. If the person were accused or charged with the crime, even if they were not convicted, a small business wouldn't know without due diligence on their part, so the cycle continues: The candidate is hired at another company and embezzles again. I've heard about this happening hundreds of times in dental offices and among other industries, and that trend alone should be a wake-up call to take important security steps.

The hope is that these checks won't take more than a few days and risk jeopardizing your hire, but it's important to stay in touch with the candidate to keep them apprised of your timeline. That communicates not only respect for their time but also your serious interest in their application.

REFERENCE CHECKS

Some people think that checking references is an outdated process, and I understand that point of view, but my guess is that they haven't seen enough bad hires to make them worthwhile. Once you have a bad experience, you see the value.

I recommend that you request at least three references from each candidate, including previous employers/supervisors and at least one former colleague or personal reference. Chances are, these self-selected references will say only positive things about the candidate, and you'll want to keep an eye out for a list that does not include the most recent employer or that gives only personal references, which can be a red flag. (It's understandable if they don't want you to call their current employer, but they should be able to give you at least one previous employer.)

You need to figure out if they are covering anything up before you offer them a job. You can ask them directly why they haven't listed a previous employer, saying something like, "I understand that you don't want me to call your current employer, but I do need to talk to someone with whom you have worked in the past. It's important if you want me to seriously consider you for this job."

If that doesn't get you anywhere, then you'll have to do a little research by checking online search engines and the candidates' social media channels and professional sites for information, keeping in mind that these were not necessarily designed for employers to see. I don't condone using that information to contact people who may be connected to your candidate's network, however, or trusting that any or all information online is true. Be cautious.

If you have been given references, schedule calls as soon as possible. Take notes during the conversation and double-check what references say against the candidate's cover letter and resume.

Here are some tips about how to proceed:

- Let the person know who you are and why you are calling, and ask how they know the candidate, in what capacity, and for how long.

- Tell them whatever you feel is needed about your position, your company, or the position the candidate is applying for, and be mindful of their time. They're doing you (and perhaps the candidate) a favor by answering your questions. You can say, "We are seriously considering [candidate's name] for a position as [title], and they will have to [cite one or two duties]. Have you seen them in a similar role? How do you think they will do as a [title]?"

- Do not share any information about the candidate with them or tell them about their experience with your hiring process. Assume that anything you tell a previous employer, colleague, or friend will get back to the candidate.

- Ask specific questions that provide insights about the candidate's abilities and that comply with the law. These include questions related to specific jobs, skills, knowledge, character, and aptitudes, as well as employment dates. Examples include the following:

  ○ Can you please verify these dates of employment and position title?

  ○ Would you consider rehiring this employee, and why or why not?

  ○ Why are they no longer working for you?

  ○ Did they get along well with others?

  ○ Did they follow directions well and meet deadlines?

  ○ Were you happy with their work?

  ○ Are they flexible? Collaborative? Empathetic?

  ○ What are their strengths and weaknesses?

  ○ Is there anything else that you'd like to share?

- Remember, it's illegal in an increasing number of states to ask about salary, salary history, or related benefits. And it's **always** illegal to ask about race/ethnic identity, religion, gender identity, sexual orientation, marital status, pregnancy or family status, age, disability, or genetic information. Be sure to check your local, state, and federal employment laws and stay updated as they evolve.

Due to limitations around communications with previous employers, doing a reference check can feel more like playing private detective. Reference checks in most cases will be more effective if you listen to *how* a past employer answers each question instead of *what* they say.

For instance, most employers will not come out and tell you that the employee stole from them, but you will be able to detect something in the tone of their voice when you ask if they would ever want to hire the candidate again. Give weight to the actual words they use, too. For example, there's a big difference between "Absolutely not!" and "Probably not."

How former employers answer your questions and their tone may give you a sense of whether they were happy with the candidate's performance. For example, if you ask them if the employee got along well with others, they might pause and offer a vague answer instead of a direct response. They might say something less positive like "Well, they tried," or they might offer an excuse for why they wouldn't hire the candidate again. They may seem like they're encouraging you to hire this person or warning you in a subtle way against that decision.

In most cases, these checks don't necessarily provide enough information to rule someone in or out, but they can reinforce the way you are already leaning. The advantage of being a small business in a community where a candidate also lives and works is that you may already be familiar with them.

Asking colleagues or mutual acquaintances about someone does not qualify as a true reference check, and I wouldn't spend too much time digging for information lest you risk losing a great candidate. If you take too long or you dig too deep, it might turn them off and make them decide to work elsewhere. But if you do have doubts about them, there's probably a good reason, and it's time to check in with your gut instinct.

Another word of caution: When a candidate is genuinely trying to hide something about their life or their past, they might go to extreme lengths to make sure you don't uncover it. That includes asking family members or friends to pose as professional references. If possible, ask for the office number of the reference so you can verify it. If any information does not check out compared to what the candidate told you or shared on their resume, then that is a huge red flag, and you need to move on to another potential hire.

BACKGROUND CHECKS

Depending on your business and the position, especially if the candidate will be working with children, older people, financial accounts, or any other sensitive information, you may want to pursue additional background checks. For some positions, a drug test might also be a smart, or required, thing to do. A background investigation can also uncover criminal convictions, motor vehicle violations, poor credit history, or false information regarding education or work history. That said, not every check is necessary for every employee or every position.

For instance, whenever I did recruiting for candidates who would be working in government agencies, background checks were always required. I also have had to hire for truck drivers, who are required to pass drug tests. Again, I would suggest you talk to an HR or legal professional who knows your industry and the relevant laws and regulations.

In a 2018 report sponsored by the National Association of Background Screeners, 95 percent of surveyed employers indicated that they use one or more types of employment background screening.[2] Eighty-five percent of employers have found misrepresentations on a resume or job application, while 77 percent have uncovered issues they wouldn't have caught otherwise, according to HireRight, an internet-based background-screening service.[3]

You can use either fee-based or free background-check services, though the latter offer more limited and sometimes inaccurate results. For fee-based services, given the time and cost involved in some of these checks, I would make sure you apply them only to your final candidates. You also need to be transparent with candidates about conducting background checks, which typically require their consent and for them to provide information such as birth dates, Social Security numbers, and current and former addresses. Some candidates may withdraw their applications, but honestly, that tells you there is something that they do not want to share, so it would not have worked out in the long run.

Having to fire someone and replace them, and falling prey to crime hits a small business much harder than a large one. Take precautions, and you'll be putting the odds of hiring success on your side.

KEY TAKEAWAYS

- Reference and background checks can be valuable ways to protect your business, employees, clients, and yourself. *It's worth exploring your candidate's background to make sure they are the hire you think they are.*

- Follow legal guidelines for reference checks. *Be aware of local, state, and federal employment regulations, and ask specific questions that are permitted within those restrictions.*

- Additional background checks may be worthwhile. *Depending on your hiring circumstances, it may be worth pursuing additional information about your final candidates. Make sure you receive their consent and use reliable sources.*

CHAPTER 10

MAKING THE OFFER

When you start planning for a new hire, it's easy to focus on how excited you are for them to join your team, instead of the reality of what they might actually bring to your company. Before extending an offer, be sure to take a moment to review your job criteria against your finalists to make sure you are not buying into a dream and ignoring reality.

What does your gut tell you? How do you really feel about them? Do you like them? Does it truly feel like the right decision or one that you are attempting to make fit your needs? Employers often ignore these feelings and decide to hire someone who checks most of the boxes. Almost every small business owner whom I have talked to about this has told me they knew someone was not a good idea from the start and eventually had to fire the person and start all over again.

Once more, take stock of the following factors for your candidates:

- **Experience.** Does their work history truly fit what you need? How much of their readiness for your role depends on your training and onboarding process? Are you willing to provide what they need to be able to get up and running in a timely manner?

- **Skills.** Do they have the key hard and soft skills necessary to succeed in the job? If they don't, are they willing and able to learn, and are you willing and able to teach them, keeping in mind that soft skills are more difficult to acquire?

- **Attitude.** Even if someone has great experience and superior skills, a bad attitude will be toxic to your company. Their interview should have shown them at their best, and if it didn't, you can expect things to only go downhill from that point.

- **Personality.** This is something, too, that is unlikely to be fixable. Can you see you, your team, and your clients working side by side and enjoying your interactions with this candidate? This doesn't mean you have to be BFFs and hang out on weekends together, but the right candidate should be compatible with your work environment and values.

- **Assessments.** Think about their references and any other background checks you performed. Are you satisfied with the outcomes?

- **Red flags.** Did your vetting process resolve any outstanding concerns you may have about this candidate? If you have two finalists, how do they compare in this respect? Do you feel more secure about hiring one over the other, given any employment gaps or the reason they left their last job? If a candidate is taking a significant pay cut, do you think they will be okay with it when they start getting their actual paycheck? (I've found some people will take jobs while they continue to look for something that pays more, or they'll start knocking on your door for a raise.) And are they excited to build a career with you, or do you get the sense a job is just a job to them? In a small business, those attitudes are felt by everyone in the workplace, affecting morale and productivity. Personally, I want to hire someone who has the highest chance of staying for a long time after I invest time and money in them.

CONSIDER YOUR OPTIONS

If you conclude that your current candidates meet a majority of these criteria, then it's time to conduct a second round of interviews or tryouts with them. If they don't, then it's time to move on and continue to look. Don't make the costly mistake of trying to make someone work out, because more often than not, it will end in failure. You went into this process trying to find your new great hire so you can grow your small business and take it to the next level. Stick to that goal. The prospect of starting again may seem tedious or painful, but I'm here to tell you that it's worth it. Even if you have an empty chair in your organization, you are better off continuing to look than hiring someone who will ultimately fail and cost you precious time and energy down the road.

If you need to go back to the start, you have a few choices at this point: You can review your current resumes or you can think about whether your job description or its placement needs to be tweaked to attract more candidates who meet your criteria. Perhaps you need to involve more people in the interviews or check additional references. What can you learn from your hiring process to make it go better the next time around?

Alternatively, you may have found that the best decision is to come up with a plan B. Maybe you've determined that the position is going to be close to impossible to fill because you need skills or qualifications that are too difficult to find in your area or industry. It may be easier to train someone on your team, and so you'll need someone new to take on their job responsibilities instead. Or the vacant position may be best filled by a contractor or by outsourcing to a third party, versus hiring a full-time employee.

Hopefully, you've crafted a focused and effective hiring process that has brought at least one great candidate to the fore, and you are ready to hire. Their experience, attitude, personality, and values meet your needs; you and your team members like them; and their references and other assessments have checked out. You don't have any serious concerns about them, and you are ready to move quickly so they don't take another job before you can extend an offer.

Of course, you won't know for sure how things will work out, but you're confident that you've put the odds of success on your side. If you have two leading candidates, be sure not to let go of one until you have gotten a yes from the other. Make sure to let the second candidate know that you will be back in touch if things change in the future, since you never know if you might end up having a role for them, too. Be sure to let everyone know the status of their applications, out of respect for them and to protect your reputation and that of your small business.

EXTEND THE OFFER

Finally! You've found the right person for your job opportunity—that's great and should make you feel good. Enjoy the moment because now it is time to offer them the job and hope they say yes.

When you reach out to them to make the offer and (in some cases) begin negotiations, be sure to follow the following guidelines:

Comply with the law. Employment regulations vary, so I recommend working with a lawyer or an HR firm or consultant to make sure you comply with local, state, and federal laws, especially in terms of your verbal and written communications with your chosen hire. Be sure to provide details about the following:

Pay. Will they receive full- or part-time pay, by the hour or salaried? Will they be eligible for bonuses or commissions or other benefits? What is the basis for pay in your workplace, and does it comply with federal law?

Disclosures. Have you told the candidate what is legally necessary in terms of their references and other background checks?

Contact the candidate in real time. You want to reach them quickly and hopefully before they receive any other offers. Good employees are generally not on the job market very long, so once you have made your decision, you want to snatch them up. You also want to hear the candidate's excitement at the offer, which should help affirm your decision. If they sound excited, seem grateful, and start to put plans in motion like figuring out start dates, then that is a great sign. Hiring is a lot of work and can seem tedious at times, so enjoy the reward of finally making an offer. However, there is still a chance you may hear hesitation or trepidation in their voice. You want to find out the reason—if they are interviewing elsewhere and where they are in that process, if they have other offers, or if they are concerned with something specific regarding your offer.

Establish terms. Reiterate the job title, status (full- or part-time, contractor, temporary-to-hire, etc.), pay rate, and start date. You don't have to go into too many other details at this point, which will be contained in a written contract and reviewed by both parties once they have accepted the position. In the meantime, you can send them a written offer to sign, and I suggest having this drawn up by a lawyer or HR professional to protect you and your employee from future disagreements.

Negotiate within your limits. Once you've established the pay rate, don't offer to pay more than you can afford in hopes of enticing the "perfect" candidate to accept the job. Instead, think creatively about ways you can bring them on, whether it's providing flextime to ensure work-life balance (which is especially important to millennials), proposing expanded telecommuting options, or offering other benefits that are important to them and still work for you.

Ask the candidate to sign an offer letter. While it should avoid language making any guarantees of future employment, such as "job security," a formal offer letter includes basic information on compensation, benefits, and any conditions of employment, such as drug tests or confidentiality agreements, as well as any documents they need to sign. It should also include the starting date, details about any trial or evaluation period, and a "please respond by" date.

POSSIBLE OUTCOMES

If your top candidate doesn't accept the offer, then you want to find out why and, if possible, try to negotiate any terms on which you differ. If that doesn't work, then graciously thank them for their time and move on. I'm sorry if that happens, because that kind of rejection, albeit professional, is like asking someone to date you and being turned down. It's worth taking a moment to consider whether you missed something in the interview process that might have told you that this would be the result. Did you take too long to get this candidate through the interview process? Was there something about your interview process that turned this candidate off from considering your company or your job? If so, is there something you can do to improve or learn from this?

Perhaps the candidate informs you that they are interested in the job but not ready to accept your offer at this point. In that case, you need to get more information and set expectations in terms of when you can expect their decision. If they are being vague or elusive, then put an expiration date on your offer so that they don't keep you waiting for too long. The best scenario is that they are transparent with you, express enthusiasm for the role, and explain why they need to delay, even if it is to say they have another offer on the table and need to weigh their choices. My experience, even then, is that they are not 100 percent fully committed to your position in the way you need them to be and, in the long run, will play this game again. You can wait forty-eight hours or even seventy-two hours, but I wouldn't suggest waiting longer than that.

In a perfect world, your top candidate accepts your position and seems as excited about working for you as you are about working with them. It's great when someone says yes on the spot. Celebrate! Enjoy the feeling! And get ready to bring them on board.

KEY TAKEAWAYS

- **Re-review your job criteria.** *Take a moment to step back and reassess whether this is, in fact, the right person for the hire. Go through your list of necessary skills and experience, among other issues, before you extend the offer.*

- **Follow guidelines when you extend the offer.** *Make sure your offer is compliant with labor regulations, contact the candidate personally to extend the offer, and gauge their reaction. Be creative but realistic when it comes to negotiations, and have a formal offer letter prepared for them to sign.*

- **Be prepared for possible outcomes.** *Depending on what happens, you may have to rethink your hiring plans or start over. It's not the end of the world, though it will certainly be a source of frustration. The good news is that you've prepared the groundwork and may have other promising candidates in the pipeline.*

CHAPTER 11

ONBOARDING YOUR NEW EMPLOYEE

Congratulations! All of your hard work has paid off. You have found a great candidate, and they've accepted your offer. You probably have a sense of relief and excitement about the future, so enjoy it. You should be happy that you found the person you hope will make your business better and help it grow.

But your job is not over. The first week or two that a new hire spends in your office is just as important as the interview process. It's an opportunity for you not only to evaluate them but also to launch them successfully in their new job. You need to make sure you are setting expectations for the candidate and your team and making provisions for the transition to go smoothly for everyone involved.

That means properly welcoming the new team member, giving them a tour of the office, making introductions, showing them where to store their belongings, and pointing out where they can find important supplies. It's also the time to get their proper paperwork, benefits, and workspace in order and to organize training either with you or a coworker. Explain and give them documentation on dress codes, office etiquette, policies, and issues such as non-business visitors and acceptable/unacceptable behavior, including sexual harassment. You'll also want to cover the following:

- Notification and consent for any alcohol or drug testing, if required

- Work hours, vacation time, overtime, unpaid time off, and sick days, among other company policies, procedures, and requirements

- Documents such as their contract, tax forms, and benefits

- Safety and security in the workplace (such as evacuation procedures) and for the employee (such as emergency contact information and any medical or food allergy information they wish to share)

- Electronics and privacy rules, including the use of personal devices and email/social media during work hours; rules around personal use of company devices; communication policies about the company; and confidentiality issues

- Office routines, including breaks, and details such as where to store and label food and keep private belongings secure (in a small business, these little details count and help everyone adjust more easily to a new person in the office)

- Anything else that is recommended by your HR company or consultant to make sure you have complied with all legal requirements

Be sure to regularly ask if your new hire has questions, and let them know your availability so they can talk to you if they do. It also helps to offer a written schedule for the first week or two of training, including some check-in meetings between the two of you. On top of that, to get their introduction off to a good start, it's a great idea to treat your new hire to a group coffee or lunch as a fun get-to-know-you session with others on the team.

TRAIN FOR SUCCESS

Many small business owners put a new hire on the job on the first day, and no one really pays attention to what they're doing. In this case, "training" is more like throwing someone into a swimming pool and waiting to see if they swim or drown. It's not efficient, effective, or fair.

The first week with a new employee is important because this is the first time you'll witness them truly on the job. It's even more important than the interview, and you need to make sure that they understand their duties and are given the best chance to succeed—which means your business succeeds, too.

By reviewing their job description and giving clear instructions, you can ensure your new hire knows what is expected of them and how to fulfill their role. It should also give them a sense of where they fit in terms of the larger mission and purpose of your business. Handbooks and checklists are also valuable, along with a contact list and description of other employees' jobs. Checklists serve as an efficient training guide to ensure the new employee understands the specifics of how to accomplish a task and doesn't miss any steps during this crucial time.

Next, give your new employee the tools they need to do their job, whether it's a computer, a phone, a particular software program, or written materials and writing implements. In our office, the No. 1 tool is the Front Office Rocks series of online training videos, which explain what happens in the front office and the specific purpose behind each task. When you're training a new hire, it's vital that they understand *why* what they are learning is important. People are more likely to be interested in learning something if they know it matters.

For example, we ask new hires to watch these videos before they begin answering the phones, so they know why handling calls and directing them correctly is important to our office. They learn what to do with each and every phone call. We once had a brand-new employee who had never been taught the importance of properly answering the phone. She watched our videos, and by day three on the job, she had converted a hard-to-schedule patient into an $8,000 dental case. She said if she had not been taught this in our office, she would not have known her purpose and how to handle the patient's situation.

Find a balance, too, between teaching your new hire a lot in the first couple of weeks and allowing them to actually grasp and apply what they learn. Teaching a new person too much at once will guarantee that they know a little bit about a lot of things but not much about anything in particular, and that means they'll miss important details and procedures. A new hire can only take in so much on the first few days and weeks; they are trying to adjust socially as well as professionally, and that can be stressful.

It's far better to spend time pacing your training in a thorough and organized way so they can absorb things bit by bit and tackle each piece successfully. People feel the need to contribute, and they'll feel good when they can, even if it is one step at a time.

Not everyone learns at the same speed or in the same way, either. Remember the "telephone game," where one person whispers in the ear of the next person, who whispers in the next person's ear, and so on? The message at the end is usually completely different from the message at the beginning. You can't assume that new employees understand everything right away, so be sure you have regular check-in points throughout training to test their ability to learn and comprehension of new tasks. Otherwise, you might just as well have thrown them in that pool.

You have to give new employees clear instructions and the tools they need. You've double-checked that they understand how to do the job, and now you need to let *them* do it. You won't have time to do your job, and the point of hiring someone to help grow your business will have been in vain. Sure, sometimes you need to go back and explain things more, but once the basic education has occurred, give them time to master each part of their role a little bit at a time.

Even after a week or two, you can't just wish them good luck and stop paying attention. In a small business, too much rides on each employee. If you assign a coworker to the new hire, make sure they are monitoring them effectively by observing, guiding as needed, and retraining when necessary. Tailor your training to fit the individual. You also need to make clear to your team members that you should be kept in the loop at all times and are willing to step in upon request.

TROUBLE SIGNS

When we put these steps in place, we hope our new employees will be off and running. However, sometimes the new employee isn't getting it, and they should be by a certain point. In our dental office, the message is that once you're hired, we consider you a part of the team, and everybody is here for the long haul. At least, that's our hope. But it doesn't always work out.

If someone is constantly asking for help after a couple of weeks and not even trying to figure things out by themselves, that's a red flag. Another red flag is if they are not asking questions at all. A negative attitude, lack of curiosity, unfriendliness, defensiveness/being inflexible, clocking in late, and leaving early are other signs that this person may not be the worthwhile investment you anticipated.

Maybe they don't have the skills you thought they did or repeatedly make the same mistakes, and those missteps can be apparent even if your new hire is working remotely. Either way, you find yourself up at night worrying about them, making excuses for them, or starting to feel annoyed by them, and that is not good for you or your business.

Most of our employees have worked for us for years, and we really love each one of them. We spend time doing fun things, which includes training and team building out of our office building—and even out of town. However, I remember one employee who had been referred by a friend. I was already getting frustrated by the questions she was asking by her second day but found myself justifying them because I really wanted to make it work with her.

Unfortunately, she didn't get any better, and after a couple of weeks, we determined it might be better to let her go sooner rather than later. I generally feel it's easier to let go of someone before getting too close to them, but every time we were about to sit down with her to start the process, she announced a family issue or emergency. Each week seemed to bring a new crisis that made us decide not to pull the plug and wait until she got through another tough situation.

After eight months, we decided there was never going to be a "good" time to let her go. By then, it was significantly harder because we had gotten to know her better and understood she had difficulties in her personal life. It made us much more stressed and exhausted by the circumstances than we would have been if we had let her go earlier.

Letting someone go will always be hard, so when you know it's inevitable, just get all of your ducks in a row and do it. In the long run, you'll be relieved, your team will more than likely support your decision and maybe thank you, and it allows the person an opportunity to move on to something that is better suited for them. I'm not advocating high turnover, but office managers and doctors and dentists tell me they knew the first week that things weren't going well with an employee and wished they had trusted their instincts then. You want to invest in your new people, train them well, and give them time to acclimate, but when there are signs that it is just not going to work, you can't let it go on forever.

If the employee doesn't work out, learn from your mistakes, talk to your team, adjust your candidate search, and move on. You don't have to start from scratch anymore because you've created a system and foundation to hire new people to grow your business.

If the new hire seems to be working out, as you expected, that's wonderful news. Continue to encourage and train them. Help them grow into their career with your small business, and watch your small business grow, too.

SIX COMMON MISTAKES

In my experience, the hardest people to successfully hire are those who serve in managerial and technical roles, whether the business is big or small. Not only is the candidate pool more limited, but the first few weeks on the job can be more challenging because there are more factors at play, from personality to hard skills. In other words, the bigger the job, the harder the fit, and often that doesn't become clear until you've got them working for you.

Nearly every small business owner trying to make one of these hires has experienced some sort of failure and disappointment. Employers can't control everything, but what I've found is that they make some common mistakes, which I want to share with you here so you can avoid them:

1. **Rushing the process.** By the time an office needs to hire a key employee, it's often too late. When you wait too long to find the right person for an important position, then the pressure

of needing someone to fill the role becomes sometimes so intense that you feel you can't afford the time to properly vet candidates. That's asking for failure. Don't try to fit the wrong person into the role, and when you find the right person, be sure to allow them the necessary time to integrate successfully into their new position. Rushing someone into fully taking over their new job without proper training can also cause them to quit, which puts you right back in the hiring mode again.

2. **Assigning too much responsibility in the beginning.** Just because you've hired someone doesn't mean that they know your office policies, culture, or procedures. It's important to avoid giving a new employee too much responsibility at the outset without giving them time to adjust and become familiar with how you do things. This burden falls to you, not your new hire. People don't know what they don't know, and it's your job to get them up to speed. A new employee can find checklists and schedules useful to navigate their way in a new job and make sure nothing is missed. At the end of the day, you want to make sure you did all that you could to help them be successful.

3. **Providing too much freedom.** This is the flip side of assigning too much responsibility, and it can be a liability, especially when new hires are nervous and trying to prove themselves. It's important to set expectations early on in terms of their decision-making power and what they are allowed to do—and what they are not. Regardless of whether the person has previous experience in a similar role, they should not have total freedom until they have learned and proven themselves. The time may come when you are more open to hearing their ideas and initiatives, but you need to have checks and

balances at the beginning to make sure that their work meets your standards and needs. Allowing them to just start working, without ensuring they are good at what they do, can lead to a lot of cleanup later. Instead, act as a facilitator to keep things moving smoothly, to avoid conflict or problems, and to let your new hire grow into a position where you feel comfortable giving them more autonomy and authority.

4. **Failing to integrate the new hire.** Regardless of their position, any new hire should be properly introduced to your team either in person or remotely, and they should receive a warm, professional welcome. Doing this is vital to their long-term success. If you just hire them and dump them into the daily schedule without properly introducing them to the team, you won't be laying the groundwork for mutual trust, acceptance, and collaboration. You'll also be depriving the team of an opportunity to bring the new hire into the fold with an accurate understanding of their experience and background and what they can bring to the workplace. When you take the time to introduce the new person in an effective and positive way, the team is more likely to speak highly of them both with each other and with patients, who are likely to follow their lead. You'll also make the new hire more comfortable, making it easier for them to start getting work done.

5. **Failing to ensure that the new hire agrees with you on key matters.** Before you hire someone, it's important to make sure that you see eye to eye when it comes to management style, client/patient treatment planning, communication, philosophies, and the particular culture, values, and mission of your small business. Leaders of any company must set the values and vision of the organization, and the expected behaviors for employees. These are what the *Huffington*

Post calls the "DNA" of a business, and it's particularly important in a small enterprise where people work closely together.[1] Of course, there's always room for discussion and interpretation of your company's "DNA" after some time, but you need to know that your employees represent you and your business and perform their functions in ways that provide consistent service and ensure your good reputation. When problems arise in this respect with a new hire, it's equally important to address them behind closed doors while showing a unified front to the team and clients/patients, unless a larger discussion is merited. You don't want someone undermining you or being perceived as undermining you, because that can threaten the entire morale and productivity of your workplace.

6. **Failing to hire someone you want to support.** Don't fall for skills and experience over everything else and miss out on someone that you can truly see grow with your business. You need to like and trust the people with whom you work and do everything you can to nurture them. Regardless of their role, you brought them in to take some of the load off of you, and hopefully they will be someone with whom you can collaborate to build your small business. Just as you expect them to back you up, you need to back them up, too. Make sure you are keeping lines of communication open and give them the opportunity to get to know you, your team, your workplace, and your clients/patients. If your new hire is a keeper—and I hope they are—then you may very well share a long and productive relationship that will bring your business the success and growth for which you've strived.

KEY TAKEAWAYS

- **Create a comprehensive onboarding system.** *Make sure you follow legal guidelines, take care of important logistics, and take steps to properly introduce your new hire to the policies and people at your office.*

- **Training takes time.** *You can set up your new hire for success by offering instructions and explanations, providing necessary tools and guidance, and giving them the opportunity to learn at their own reasonable pace.*

- **Proceed with caution.** *Keep an eye out for trouble signs from your new employee but also make sure you don't rush training or assign too much responsibility at first, among other common employer mistakes.*

FINAL THOUGHTS

As we wrap up, I'd like to leave you with this strategy: Think of your best employee, either current or past, and your workplace before you hired them. Consider why you value them and what they have done to help your business. What would your business be without them? That great employee helped you get to where you are today, and their positive impact began when you made the decision to hire them. Thank goodness you did, right? This is what you need to imagine as you build your business: Your next best employee is out there, just waiting for you to find them.

People are often afraid of change, but I learned a long time ago that the only thing that remains the same in life *is* change. Things change, people change, businesses change, and as a result, we need to adapt and grow. Change often means replacing or hiring new employees. The sooner you embrace it, the sooner you can build a team you love with a strong hiring process that brings the best out in everyone and moves your business forward.

I totally understand the desire to stay in your comfort zone and refuse to face the unknown or risk failure. Don't rock the boat, we tell ourselves. Be comfortable. But change does not allow for that, and following the principles of this book and learning how to hire well will prepare you and your business to meet the challenges of growth head-on.

Adopting a positive attitude about hiring, developing an efficient and effective process, and starting new hires out on the right foot is all part of the journey. Thank you for going on that journey with me, and I am confident that with these lessons, some determination, and a little luck (because there's always a little luck involved), you'll find your next rock star.

ACKNOWLEDGMENTS

Nicole, you have been waiting for this book for years, and it is finally here. I want to thank you for all of your help and support in getting this out. You know that the world needs help hiring, and I appreciate all of your many hours helping me to get this done! You are a true rock star.

Drew K., you were the boss who showed me what I wanted to be when I grew up. You taught me so much, not only about recruiting but also about how to be a cool boss. I can't thank you enough for all of your support and guidance.

NOTES

CHAPTER 1

1. "More Than Half of Surveyed US Small Business Owners Recognize the Risks of Making the Wrong Hire," Monster.com (Press Room), May 3, 2016, https://www.monster.com/about/a/more-than-half-of-surveyed-u-s-small-business-owners-recognize-the-risks-of-making-the-wrong-hire.

2. Ben Goldberg, "75% of Employers Have Hired the Wrong Person, Here's How to Prevent That," CareerBuilder, November 17, 2016, https://resources.careerbuilder.com/news-research/prevent-hiring-the-wrong-person.

3. Monster.com, "More Than Half of Surveyed US Small Business Owners."

CHAPTER 2

1. Greg McKeown, "Hire Slow, Fire Fast," *Harvard Business Review*, March 3, 2014, https://hbr.org/amp/2014/03/hire-slow-fire-fast.

2. John Coleman, "Six Components of a Great Corporate Culture," *Harvard Business Review*, May 6, 2013, https://hbr.org/2013/05/six-components-of-culture.

CHAPTER 3

1. "How to Avoid a Bad Hire," UVM Today (blog), February 13, 2015, https://www.uvm.edu/uvmnews/news/how-avoid-bad-hire.

2. Brian Westfall, "Effect of Visual Job Listings Content on Applicants," Software Advice, October 9, 2014, https://www.softwareadvice.com/hr/industryview/visual-job-postings-2014.

3. William C. Dunkelberg and Holly Wade, "NFIB Small Business Economic Trends," National Federation of Independent Business, January 2018, https://www.nfib.com/assets/SBET-January-2018-1.pdf.

CHAPTER 4

1. Kathryn Dill, "Employee Referrals Lead to More Successful Job Matches," *Forbes*, August 13, 2015, https://www.forbes.com/sites/kathryndill/2015/08/13/employee-referrals-lead-to-more-successful-job-matches/#5434b0e62291.

CHAPTER 7

1. Lauren Feiner, "Coronavirus Devastating Small Businesses: One-Third Won't Reopen, 55% Won't Rehire Same Workers, Facebook Study Finds," CNBC, May 18, 2020, https://www.cnbc.com/2020/05/18/facebook-survey-details-coronavirus-small-business-devastation.html.

CHAPTER 8

1. Aleks Peterson, "Consider These Costs Before Hiring a New Employee," Fast Company, October 12, 2018, https://www.fastcompany.com/90250227/consider-these-costs-before-hiring-a-new-employee.

CHAPTER 9

1. Monster.com, "More Than Half of Surveyed US Small Business Owners."

2. Thomas Ahearn, "NAPBS Survey Reveals 95 Percent of Employers Conducting Employment Background Screening in 2018," Employment Screening Resources (blog), July 2, 2018, https://www.esrcheck.com/wordpress/2018/07/02/napbs-survey-reveals-95-percent-employers-conducting-employment-background-screening-2018.

3. "Background Checks: Intelligent Solutions for Employment Screening," HireRight, https://www.hireright.com/background-checks.

CHAPTER 11

1. Scott MacFarland, "Why Should Companies and Employees Have Shared Values?" *Huffington Post*, November 6, 2013, https://www.huffpost.com/entry/why-should-companies-and-_b_4225199.

INDEX

ABOUT THE AUTHOR

LAURA NELSON is the founder of Front Office Rocks™, a virtual training platform for dental teams that teaches office systems and methods to help practices achieve exceptional customer service.

With her interactive and innovative approach as the leader in dental front office solutions and training, Laura has mentored thousands of dentists, business owners, and dental team members to help them achieve unprecedented results in growth and empower small business owners to excel at performance-based hiring.

An accomplished recruiting and management coach and renowned keynote speaker, she is the best-selling author of *Step Away from the*

Drill, a book that has helped dentists understand and embrace the business side of dentistry. Laura received her undergraduate degree in human resources from Eastern Michigan University and her master's degree in organizational leadership from Johns Hopkins University, where she focused on leadership development and success. She is a member of the National Speakers Association, the Speaking Consulting Network, and the Academy of Dental Management Consultants, and a Fellow of the American Association of Dental Office Management.

Laura has received public-speaking awards from the Speaking Consulting Network and Dentistry's Got Talent and has also been recognized as one of *Dental Products Report*'s Top 25 Women in Dentistry.

Laura lives in Coronado, California, with her amazing husband, Chris. She has two adult children and three beautiful bonus stepdaughters. Laura enjoys spending time traveling and exploring new destinations with her husband and family. She has accomplished multiple Spartan races and enjoys biking and is always looking to learn and grow and help others in their journeys.

CONNECT WITH LAURA:

FACEBOOK: www.facebook.com/LauraNelsonSpeakerAuthor

INSTAGRAM: www.instagram.com/lauranelsonspeaks

LINKEDIN: www.linkedin.com/in/laura-nelson-speaks-9473061ba

WEBSITE: www.lauranelsonspeaks.com

Made in the USA
Las Vegas, NV
27 January 2021